AWAKENED

the Account of David Anderson

A man miraculously awakened from certain brain death and left with complete amnesia...

...to rebuild his life, relationships and marriage.

AWAKENED

DONNA BRODLAND
AS TOLD BY JOAN ANDERSON

© 1998 by Donna Brodland. All rights reserved

Printed in the United States of America

Packaged by WinePress Publishing, PO Box 1406, Mukilteo, WA 98275. The views expressed or implied in this work do not necessarily reflect those of WinePress Publishing. Ultimate design, content, and editorial accuracy of this work is the responsibility of the author(s).

No part of this publication may be reproduced, stored in a retrieval system, or transmitted in any way by any means—electronic, mechanical, photocopy, recording or otherwise—without the prior permission of the copyright holder, except as provided by USA copyright law.

Scripture quotations are taken from the New King James Version, Copyright © 1979, 1980, 1982 by Thomas Nelson, Inc., Publishers. Used by permission.

ISBN 1-57921-127-5
Library of Congress Catalog Card Number: 98-60794

Special Thanks from David and Joan Anderson

- To our lovely daughter, Donna Brodland, for all the hours she spent gathering our thoughts and writing the manuscript that would become *Awakened*. Thank you for your hard work and enthusiasm for each page. We love you, Donna!
- To the rest of our children—Doreen, Susan, and Scott—for all their input and encouragement. Thank you!

Thanks from Donna Brodland

- To my husband, Sam Brodland, for the time, energy, and editing help he brought to this project. This manuscript would not be complete without him.
- To my children, Keith and Jessica, for not feeling neglected while Mommy spent many hours at the computer.
- To all my family members, for proofreading this manuscript again and again and for their constant encouragement. Thank you!
- To my parents, David and Joan Anderson, for teaching me by example that I can praise the Lord, no matter what comes my way.

Foreword from Dr. Thor W. Stebeck

It is an honor to write this brief introduction for my good friends David and Joan Anderson. They went through an extraordinary experience, and with honesty and frankness Joan relates their story.

You will enjoy reading this book. This is a living testimony of God's mercy and grace in the recovery of both David and Joan from this tragic event.

Awakened is a story of miracle after miracle, the story of two individuals being melted, molded, motivated, and moved by the Great Creator Himself. It is a living example of God and man, and how He cares for those who trust Him.

The story continues as the lives of these two precious people go on, still under the direction of God Himself. In this book, Joan Anderson reveals the tender care of God's protective love in her family. . . . Your heart will be stirred. Donna Brodland has done an excellent job in writing this remarkable story as told by her mother.

—*Dr. Thor W. Stebeck*
Minister of Pastoral Care
Cedar Park Assembly of God, Bothell, Washington
Pastor of the church where the Anderson Family was ministering
in the prologue and epilogue

Foreword from Rev. David F. Harrison

It is a beautiful evening, and we are looking out the window of our apartment on Phinney Avenue. Just a few minutes ago I finished the book *Awakened*, the true and miraculous story of the builder and owner of this building. David G. B. Anderson has been my friend since childhood, and yet I never fully understood the miracle of his "healing" and the depth of the Anderson family's trial and triumph until now!

My wife and I were a part of the mission team that David led to Brazil in 1964. The lives of all the young people on that mission were forever changed. Three of us have since dedicated our lives as missionaries to Brazil, and all of the team are active in ministry until this day.

I have been one of those friends who unintentionally has caused the Anderson family to grieve by expecting David to remember a shared experience that was erased from his memory by his illness, but who has marveled at the gifts that God restored miraculously!

This is a book that will encourage every believer in Christ and will positively influence anyone who is seeking to know if God is real and cares about His children!

Donna Brodland has portrayed a beautiful picture of her parents' most severe trial in *Awakened*.

—Rev. David F. Harrison
Missionary to Brazil, Assemblies of God
Member of 1964 ministry team to Brazil led by David

Foreword from Bud Tutmarc

I've known Dave Anderson for many, many years. Almost all of our association has been centered around music—recording, orchestras, choirs, etc. Both he and his wife, Joan, and their lovely family have been loving and serving God as the core of their lives. It wasn't until I read this manuscript that I fully realized what a truly trying and difficult experience they had gone through, and at such a young age. It was truly the grace of God and their faith and strength of character that brought them through this devastating period and shaped them into an even stronger couple that relies totally on God for each step of their lives.

How like God to bring even a troubled, difficult mother-in-law relationship to a sweet, peaceful ending. Joan is to be commended for holding steady under pressure so God could do His miracle.

This book will hold your attention and be interesting as well as imparting some life lessons.

—Bud Tutmarc
Minister of music, recording artist
Producer of the Horizon Sound's first three recordings

Foreword from Ray and Evelyn Erickson

. . . We have recalled with vivid memories those dark, trying days the Anderson family went through. With every turn of the page we have cried, laughed, and relived the events day by day described in *Awakened*. The prayer-filled nights, the trust that came and, yes, the waves of doubt and helplessness that we also felt so keenly during that time. Then the miraculous events to follow of David's healing and victory as they reached out in faith to God.

This is an exciting book of trust in the midst of a raging storm. You will be blessed, encouraged, and enlightened with the reality of Christ's great love for His children, His almighty power, and His provision for every need known to mankind. As you read this beautifully written, true story, your heart will be drawn closer to our wonderful Lord.

—Ray and Evelyn Erickson
Close friends of David and Joan during David's illness

Prologue

Music permeated the room. Hands clapped in enthusiastic rhythm. Worship to the Lord was powerful as the gymnasium full of singing kids and their families praised God in unison. They were there to receive recognition for their achievements in the Missionette/Royal Ranger program for the school year of 1975–76. Anticipation was mounting, and I could feel their excitement; the electric atmosphere was contagious.

I glanced to my right. My three teenage daughters—Doreen, Donna, and Susan—were quietly singing in worship with the gathering of young people. I smiled inwardly at their less-than-enthusiastic tones; the result of a severe case of preconcert jitters. I wasn't concerned, because I knew once they began performing, their voices would ring clear and true, praising our Lord in song. In fact, their nervousness was due mostly to the fact each one had to introduce one of our musical numbers. The idea of talking in front of a crowd always had their palms sweating and their hearts skipping beats.

The music died down as the song came to a close and the pastor of the church stepped to the podium to make some announcements and hand out awards. I moved my head to watch him as he spoke, and out of the corner of my eye I noticed Scott, my five-year-old son, squirming in his seat. A bundle of pent-up energy, he wasn't one for sitting still for

Prologue

any length of time. I placed my hand gently on his knee to catch his attention, silently communicating his need to sit quietly.

His blue eyes beseechingly looked up at me, eyes so like his father's, but eyes that were now pleading for mercy as he shifted impatiently in his seat.

A brief, nostalgic smile touched my lips. Scott's energy and enthusiasm reminded me of David, my husband, when he was younger: a go-getter mixed with a dash of dreamer and just a touch of impatience.

As the pastor continued passing out awards, I glanced over to where David was sitting. He was seriously intent on his little brown notebook, studying the words of the songs we were going to sing. I watched as the signs of tension built around his temple: His brow furrowed, and his hand crept up to gently massage the deepening creases. The pressure of remembering the lyrics of the songs we were going to sing, as well as the responsibility for organizing the performance, weighed heavily on him.

As I continued my scrutiny, David's eyes lifted and met mine. In one brief moment, he communicated his fears to me. He visibly swallowed, a telling sign that he was nervous about sharing his testimony with the assembled crowd.

Instantly, the details of David's story flashed through my head: David becoming so sick with a virus that he was hospitalized. . . . The fever searing his mind to such a degree that he went into delirium . . . then waking up from his mentally unconscious state, without memory—complete amnesia . . .

My flashback skidded to a stop. I knew David's amnesia was the cause of his nervousness. Every time he talked about his past he had to rely completely on second-hand history. The only specifics he knew about the events before and during his illness were based on what other people had told him. His past wasn't just a blur, it was gone—a blank. Most people couldn't understand that one day he woke up, a twenty-nine-year-old man with no memory of his past.

As David's eyes held mine, I smiled, my confidence in him adding a special glow. David's gaze dropped, landing on our Bible sitting on the seat between us. Slowly, the apprehension began to ease from his features as the book reminded him of God's unfailing intervention in our lives.

The tension lifted, and a faint smile curved around David's lips. His expression softened as he inwardly focused on Jesus, drawing comfort and strength. Wonder and appreciation filled his gaze, lighting from

Prologue

within. He slowly shut his eyelids. I knew that David would worry no longer. He had turned the service over to God.

After the last round of applause for the awards died away, I heard the pastor introduce us, *The Horizon Sounds* by the Anderson Family. We were the featured guests for this special event. I felt my heart jump slightly; adrenaline pumped into my bloodstream, leaving my palms wet and my throat dry. In my peripheral vision, I saw my daughters stand and begin to move, single file, to the front of the room. I stood and David moved to my side. He placed his hand on the small of my back and pushed ever so slightly, loosening my legs to step toward the platform.

My body began to tremble slightly—nerves, excitement? I could feel the warm energy radiating from David to me. I felt him shiver, excited now that another moment had come to share his life and his love for God. Supernatural confidence exuded from his touch. David was ready to convey the joy and the sorrow, the pain and the triumph in learning to praise the Lord in song.

The crowd of young people grew quieter as the five of us picked up our multicolored microphones. We stood in a row, dressed alike in maroon and white, and prepared to sing.

As the music began, I swallowed, trying to rid my voice of any tremor. Finally, the cue arrived and we sang.

As each song echoed through the building, I breathed a little easier. Our songs of praise were rising higher and higher, reaching into heaven, expressing our thoughts, our feelings, our hopes. The words of our song resounded:

> No more tears when we get to heaven,
> No more pain when we get to heaven,
> No more war when we get to heaven,
> No more death![1]

Prologue

David sung those lyrics from the heart because they expressed what was in the core of his soul. They graphically described what he had experienced more than ten years before. Music and emotion danced together. The feeling of what heaven would be like was projected to the listeners as we sang.

The girls stepped forward to sing a trio. They sang the words with confidence, the message ringing clear:

> Do you want a life of action,
> And a sense of satisfaction?
> Take the life Christ offers now and live.
> Really live. [2]

The kids in the gymnasium clapped when they were done. I prayed that the words of the song would be real in their hearts, that they would take what Jesus had to offer: life everlasting.

It was time now for David and I to sing a duet. We sang an ageless hymn, an old favorite with a unique arrangement of melody and counterpart that highlighted David's strong baritone and my high soprano range. "The Old Rugged Cross" rang out across the congregation. Some of the older parents and grandparents in the crowd wiped away tears. Even some of the younger listeners sat enthralled as the words described what the Lord Jesus had endured for our salvation and for our healing.

All five of us gathered together again for our final song. An arrangement of "Blessed Assurance" reached out over the listeners, the hope and promise of the words stirring every heart and lifting my spirit:

> This is my story,
> This is my song,
> Praising my Savior all the day long. [3]

The words touched my heart as I sang. The song expressed exactly what the Lord had given David and I to do: to praise Him all day, every day.

Praise to Jesus filled my heart and soul, surrounding me and blessing me. My previous tension was now completely obliterated by the presence of God Himself, His Spirit touching every word and every sound.

Prologue

The song came to a close; the light swing of the music lingered in the air and cloaked the atmosphere with peace. As quiet descended, no one stirred. The silence was electrified, charged with unspoken awe. Then, throughout the congregation softly whispered words of heavenly praise slowly became audible, ascending to the only one deserving of our adoration, "Praise the Lord. . . ."

"Thank you, Jesus. . . ."

"I love you, Lord. . . ."

David turned his head to look at me, his glance communicating that he was ready to speak. I gave him an encouraging smile as I turned to leave the platform. Moving toward my daughters, I signaled our exit to them. We quietly filed to our seats.

David stepped forward and began to speak, his anxiety completely gone. The crowd of young people became a little restless, I figured they were settling in for "a sermon preached by a musician." I smiled confidently to myself as I thought about what their reaction to David's story would likely be.

David began to unfold the events of a decade ago that led up to his miraculous awakening, and the congregation hushed. No more restless movement disturbed the calmness. Hands sat motionless; lips were silent. All eyes were on David; all ears strained for his next word.

I knew the story by heart now; I had lived it. So I looked around at the kaleidoscope of faces hearing David's words for the first time. Attention focused completely on him; they were captivated by his story: David thrashing in delirium . . . the doctors giving up . . . his healing . . . the doctor telling him of his life—the life of which he had no memory. But suddenly my attention was arrested as David's words took a turn I had never heard before.

David was intent on what he was saying. His eyes were focused on no one in particular as he struggled to relive his first thoughts and feelings of waking up without memory over ten years ago, struggling to explain how he had felt.

"The doctor was trying to explain to me who I was and what had happened to me, when the door opened," he said. "I glanced up expecting to see just another person dressed in hospital white but, instead, in walked a young woman dressed in wonderful color—everything but white." The crowd chuckled in amusement as he continued. "To my eyes, she was the most beautiful thing I had ever seen."

Prologue

David paused briefly in his testimony and smiled at me. His eyes twinkled with joy and love, reliving the moment of that meeting. I was intrigued. David had never before included this part of his story. I leaned forward in my seat ever so slightly. Curious, I waited for David to continue.

David returned his gaze to the congregation and continued. "I turned to the doctor, interrupting him in mid-sentence. 'Who is she?' I whispered.

"The doctor abruptly shifted his gaze to look over at the woman who had just entered the room, and immediately lowered his voice so only I could hear him. 'That young lady,' he said, 'is your *wife*.'"

I stared at David in disbelief. He continued his testimony, totally oblivious to the fact that he had just dropped a bomb on me. I sat stiffly in my seat, frozen in time, with the words "that young lady is your wife" repeatedly echoing in my head. *That young lady is your wife?!*

I was numb. Slowly, I tried to make some sense of his words. They swirled out of focus in my mind. Their meaning was just out of reach, beyond my grasp. The doctor had told David who *I* was.

Was David really saying that he had not known me? Was *I* as much a stranger to David as the girls . . . as his mother, father, and other relatives had been?

Spontaneously, images and memories began to rise out of the fog of confusion. Pictures of the past, including David's illness, formed in my mind's eye—bringing the truth of the past into focus.

Chapter One

I was born in 1937 to John and Connie Franz. We lived in Middletown, a small town in upper New York State. My father was trained to operate weaving machines and worked for Middletown Knitting Mill. In the early 1950s, jobs dried up and the small town began to fizzle. My dad, correctly predicting the death of the community, packed up his family of six and moved out West. We arrived in Seattle, Washington, in 1952, and my dad was employed at a local knitting factory.

The economic environment of the early '50s pressured my mom to get a job although she was a stay-at-home mom at heart. She waited tables, checked groceries, and even tried her hand at being a beautician. My sister and I also got jobs. I baby-sat two small boys a couple days a week, juggling my schedule around school and work. I helped around the house by cooking, cleaning, and watching my younger brother. I also went to church. Every Sunday we were sent to Sunday school and then we were joined by Mom for Sunday service. Our weekly lessons at church taught us the basic golden rules of Christianity: (1) Jesus loves me and (2) Love your neighbor as yourself. But the idea of having an intimate relationship with Jesus Christ was never even addressed.

My dad loved music—jazz and big-band styles were his favorite. He spent most of his weekend nights moonlighting in dance clubs; his mellow saxophone tones blending with the rest of his band. This schedule kept him too tired to attend church on a regular basis.

Dad's music birthed in me a love to dance. On special occasions, my older sister and I would go with Dad to the club. There we could dance with the patrons while my dad kept a close eye on us from the stage. We would swing our midcalf skirts around to the tunes and clap our hands in rhythm, laughing and loving the feel of the music. I also loved to sing. In fact, when I started high school, the first class I signed up for was choir.

God ordained my footsteps and orchestrated my direction by placing me in Ballard High School's Concert Choir. This choir was assisted by the school's most promising, upcoming student director: David Anderson.

David was born in 1936 to Eric and Helen Anderson, the second of two sons. He was born in Seattle, Washington, in the Ballard neighborhood, often referred to as "Little Scandinavia."

Eric was a Swedish immigrant who came to America, the "Land of Opportunity," at the age of sixteen. His trek got him as far as Seattle, where he had friends who gave him a job and a place to stay.

Helen was born to Swedish immigrants and grew up on a farm in North Dakota. She taught school in her late teens and later trained to be a nurse.

Eric partnered in the construction trade with his friends, who were relatives of Helen's. The two met on one of Helen's trips to Seattle to visit her relatives.

Eric and Helen were married in 1933. However, on her wedding night, Helen learned that Eric had lost everything in what would later be known as the Great Depression. He informed her that he was "head over heels" in debt. Stunned by the truth and unwilling to share in his indebtedness, Helen walked out on Eric. For several days she wrestled with her choice: honor her personal commitment to being debt-free or honor her marriage vows. Her commitment to Eric prevailed, but serious tension remained in their relationship. Helen's confidence in her new husband's ability to provide was broken.

Helen's independent, strong-willed disposition wouldn't let her rest until all their debts were paid. She worked nights while Eric worked

Chapter One

days, struggling to pay back every borrowed cent. During this time, Helen gave birth to her first son. Then two years later in 1936, David was born, adding yet another mouth to feed.

Over time, the debts were paid and Eric's construction business became financially solvent again. Still, Helen worked whenever she could. She refused to give up her independence or to rely on anyone else. She knew firsthand how easy it was to lose everything in a heartbeat—or in an "I do."

Eric quietly lead the home and only occasionally would feel the need to assert his authority. Yet, Helen struggled in her submission to his leadership. She pushed against the restraints of husband and children; and, at times, her frustration level would peak with an eruption of anger.

Helen was a black-and-white kind of a person. Any given situation was either good or bad—nothing in between. She would cling to her point of view, and nothing could sway her from her given perception. This stubborn, robust nature supported her through some rough times in her childhood and through the Depression, but those same characteristics made keeping a consistently close relationship with her family virtually impossible.

David was restricted to an extremely confining schedule. He studied piano, violin, and voice. Eric and Helen were also avid churchgoers. Between two churches, the family attended three services every Sunday, one service on Saturday, and other meetings during the week as well. Between school, practice sessions, and church, there was little time for a social life.

David, an accomplished violinist

Helen also tried to control David's social life, going so far as to decide with whom he could be friends. She even tried pushing her choice of girlfriends on David. She set up dates and encouraged relationships with certain girls from their church. One time David complied with her choice, but David cut the date short when the girl started unbuttoning her own blouse. This was not the

Awakened

kind of "Christian" girl David was interested in dating.

As one might imagine, instead of the control and regulation Helen craved, her domineering dictatorship caused a form of quiet rebellion. David internalized the conflict; his body created an ulcer as early as age twelve. He isolated himself from the family and retreated from social life. He became a loner and channeled his energy into music.

By the time David reached high school he was an accomplished musician. He could play the piano very well, and his violin playing was described as "gifted." But David's real love was conducting. Directing many musicians and blending them into one, unified sound was his ambition. His talent matured until he became the musical star of his high school. God ordained David's footsteps and orchestrated his direction, placing him in front of Ballard High School's Concert Choir—a choir that had me sitting in the soprano section.

Outside of school David and I had nothing in common. At Ballard High, David was one grade ahead of me, and we ran in different social circles. But God put us both in concert choir. To say we saw each other across the room and fell madly in love would be overstating the truth just a bit, but I do remember admiring David. I remember sitting in music class and watching this cute, older guy directing the choir. David was charming and attractive, with a bright, wide smile. His forehead would crinkle in concentration as he would lean over the conductor's stand during practice; and his whole face would light up when the singers responded correctly to one of his flamboyant cues. His arms moved smoothly and effortlessly to the music, punctuating every beat and nuance of the musical piece. Every eye in the chorus was pulled by his charisma, and we responded as one to his animated gestures.

David would stand in front of us, leaning back on his heels just slightly and listening intently. Sometimes his eyes would briefly close as he savored the harmony surrounding him. Then they would flutter open again, bright and sparkling, and his ever-present grin would widen. He loved the music, the harmony, and being immersed in the sound that flowed from our vocal force.

I loved choir and I admired David. His talent; his dark, wavy hair streaked with golden highlights; his blue eyes that twinkled with enthu-

Chapter One

siasm and humor; his charismatic personality; his Christianlike manners; and his contagious smile were packaged together in a slim, athletically built young man. The combination presented all the right ingredients for drawing admirers. Yet, David was a loner, almost unapproachable when not in front of the chorus.

As for me, I went to school and associated with my small circle of close friends. I went to class and went home. I had a boyfriend, but I was planning to call off the relationship.

I considered myself shy and unassuming. I was "one among the crowd" of sopranos in the choir. I had shoulder-length, dark blond hair with a slight bounce of natural curl. But in my opinion, I was not outstanding or eye-catching. I had blue eyes and wore lipstick, and I dressed just like everyone else did in 1954—midcalf-length wool skirts, short-sleeved sweaters, bobby socks, and saddle shoes. In short, I blended in.

David, age 19

Consequently, you could have knocked my bobby socks off the day David called me for a date. . . .

It was Friday, and I was glad to be going home. Cool shadows and warm light made me certain it was springtime as my steps drew me closer to the house. A bird fluttered its wings and chirped happily from above my head, and a slight spring breeze gently touched my cheek. The floating wind mildly brushed the flowering daffodils regally lining our front walk and caused them to sway. I ran past the blossoms and up the front steps.

I walked in the front door and let it close behind me. The house was quiet; Mom and Dad were working, and my sisters were not home yet.

Once in my room, I kicked off my saddle shoes and threw them into the closet. I dragged a pair of trousers out of my wardrobe, dropped my skirt, and hitched the pants up around my waist.

I flopped onto my bed and began to organize my homework.

Faintly, I heard the sound of the phone ring.

Awakened

Rolling off my bed, I dashed to the door. The phone rang twice more as I scrambled down the stairs.

Out of breath, I reached the phone extension in the living room and grabbed the receiver.

"Hello," I panted.

Silence greeted my ear. Then, faintly, I heard a throat clear and someone began to speak.

"Is this Joan Franz?" A low, hesitant, masculine voice crackled in the receiver. The unfamiliar male voice sparked a teenage flutter of nerves.

Who? I wondered.

I took a deep, calming breath and forced a reply.

"Yes," I gulped. I moistened my dry lips.

Again the voice was cleared. "This is . . . I'm not sure if you know who I am, but this is David Anderson. I, umm . . . well, I'm in choir with you, and I was wondering if you would be interested in . . ."

There was a slight hesitation in the voice.

". . . in maybe going to a concert with me tonight."

My heart somersaulted, my pulse went into double-time. I couldn't believe it! David Anderson was asking me out tonight!

Oh no, I winced. My euphoria was immediately destroyed with the intrusion of reality. I couldn't go. Even though it was going to be our last date, I had already promised to go out with someone else. I was devastated, and I groaned inwardly. At least, I hope it was inside, because the next thing David said made me wonder if he had heard me.

"If you're busy or would rather not, that's OK," he politely gave me an easy way to refuse.

"No, David, I mean, yes, I would really like to go out with you, but . . . but I have other plans for tonight," I finally admitted. I was frightened my words would abruptly end our conversation.

There was a scant pause, and then he whispered, "Oh."

Tension and disappointment crackled in the silence, neither one of us knew quite what to say. I wanted to scream into the receiver, *Don't hang up!* and to beg *Please, please ask me out another time!* But he remained disappointingly silent.

I took a deep breath and swallowed, trying to rid my voice of any tremor. Gingerly, I spoke into the awkward silence.

"I'm sorry I have other plans tonight, but is the concert playing tomorrow night as well?"

Chapter One

I cringed and scolded, *Well you've done it now, Joan. You've thrown yourself at this dreamboat. He's never going to call you again, that's for sure.* I was so consumed with reprimanding myself that I almost didn't hear David's sigh or the beginning of his response.

"No, the concert is only playing tonight, but . . ." his voice grew in confidence, "we could do something different tomorrow."

His voice paused, I could almost hear his mind running through a list of possible date activities, and I held my breath, waiting and praying for him to think of something.

"How about going to the boat show on Lake Washington together? It's the first day of boating season, and everyone with or without webbed feet turns out." He laughed confidently.

The air escaped my lungs in a sudden rush.

I couldn't believe it. I was stunned and dazed, yet somehow I was able to stammer an answer.

"That sounds very nice."

"Great, I'll pick you up at ten."

"OK."

"See you then!"

"Bye."

The phone went dead in my ear. I was paralyzed, my sixteen-year-old stomach churning from the emotions coursing through me. I stood motionless for several seconds, minutes—I'm not sure how long—but gradually I realized I was still clutching the phone. I set the receiver back in its cradle; a wistful smile played at my lips.

I could still hear David's last words echoing in my ear, *Great, I'll pick you up at ten.* I could visualize the smile on his face when he said those words just by the tone of his voice. His low, jubilant voice had reverberated with anticipation. He actually sounded happy and excited to be going out with me.

I couldn't believe it! I, Joan Franz, was going on a date with the elusive catch, the talented David Anderson!

Our first date was a success. David was wonderful. We laughed together and talked, and during that day at Lake Washington we quickly became best friends.

Awakened

David and I dated throughout the remainder of David's senior year at Ballard High School and throughout the next year as well—my senior year.

As each day went by, I realized more and more that our relationship was special. It didn't matter what we did or where we went, I was just happy to be with David. We could just sit and talk for hours and I would be content. I was never bored. David listened to me talk, and I listened to him. And we began to fall more and more in love with each other.

David shared his dreams and his ambitions with me. He talked about music, and he talked about carpentry. He loved to work with his hands, to build and create things; yet, he also loved music. He was pulled in two directions at once. He had a music scholarship available to him, but he believed that registering in the University of Washington's School of Engineering would be much more practical. He struggled with these decisions and discussed them with me.

David also revealed some of the problems he was facing at home. He explained the pressure and demands that were placed on him and the controlling influence of his mother. Yet, he barely touched on what our relationship was doing to his home life. David downplayed the fact that our relationship was creating tension in his home, but he did explain that his mother was not too happy with me. David laughed when he gave me the reason: My father played in nightclubs. I didn't take the threat of her dislike too seriously; she was a bit reserved but always kind to me.

David rebelled against the parameters set by his parents. He began doing some of the things he had been brought up to avoid, but he never even hinted that he was being disobedient. To please me, we went to movies together and even attended his senior prom—amusements I thought were part of normal living. But David was chafing under the guilt of doing these activities.

Then, on one date, we were walking out of a movie theater and David's parents happened to drive by the entrance. Panicking, David grabbed my arm and shoved me back through the door.

"We're going this way," he panted as I stumbled after him.

We ran through the lobby and out the side door to the alley, narrowly avoiding exposure.

I was stunned.

Later, in the car, David explained for the first time that he was not supposed to go to movies. He told me that he felt guilty every time he walked through a theater doorway, and he couldn't do it anymore.

Chapter One

As soon as my surprise abated, I responded. "It's OK, David. We don't need to go. . . . I just want to be with you."

David told me that he had not only been rebelling against the restraints dictated by his parents, but he had also been running from God as well. He was tired of running, and he wanted his relationship with Jesus back to normal.

We prayed.

After that night, our conversations had a new focus. Jesus Christ became the center of our relationship.

Being with David was changing my life. I was a Christian and I loved Jesus, but Christianity had never been a one-on-one personal relationship with the Son of God.

Each date brought David and me closer. Our discussions helped me to understand David and to learn his personality. Every conversation also led to a deeper understanding of who God was and how Jesus could be in every part of my life.

If anyone knew anything about the Bible, it was David. He had memorized scriptures, and he read it regularly. The thing that was incredible to me was the way he talked about the Bible. He made it fascinating. Before I had known David, the Bible had just been another book to me, but through David's eyes, the Bible had come alive. The way he explained the amazing truths and promises that were in God's Word and that they were actually available to me was mind-boggling.

At the time I didn't realize it, but the Holy Spirit was using David to teach me. The Holy Spirit was opening my heart and helping me to understand what God wanted to say to me. David had become my spiritual leader, my mentor, my teacher. And through David and his love for Jesus Christ, I was learning to know and love David's God as well. Jesus was now my closest friend—a personal relationship I had never expected to have with God Almighty.

David brought me to his church, a Pentecostal, full-gospel congregation. This was definitely a new experience for me. Not only did they teach God's Word in a way I had never heard before, but they also taught about the Holy Spirit and how to live and walk in a Spirit-filled life. At first, this confused me and even scared me a little. The services were different than anything I had previously experienced. People in the congregation raised their hands while they sang in worship, and they actually prayed out loud in a seemingly chaotic way, each member speaking

Awakened

in agreement to the person leading in prayer. At times, it was so loud it was hard to hear what the praying person was saying. "Hallelujah's," "Praise the Lord's," and "Amen's" mingled and intertwined with speaking in tongues; the noise filled the room.

My confusion and apprehension were removed by David. He showed me the scripture in Acts 2:4, "And they were all filled with the Holy Spirit and began to speak with other tongues, as the Spirit gave them utterance." I was seeing touches of the same thing in David's church, and I wanted to be a part of it.

Changes began to be evident in my daily conduct. Devotions became a daily routine. I talked to Jesus constantly; He became my best friend. Even my outward appearance changed. One outward commitment I made was dropping my use of lipstick. Did that ever create an uproar in my house! My family said I looked like I was sick all the time, and I was nicknamed "Blue Lips." But the ridicule seemed manageable and definitely worth enduring when I knew I was taking a step in what I believed to be obedience to the Lord.

God's providential hand intervened in my life. He brought David and me together, and David opened up a whole new world for me, a life of walking in obedience and submission to the Spirit of God.

As my senior year in high school neared its conclusion, I began to think about what to do after graduation. Every option that rose to my mind had one common thread: They all included David. After a year of dating David, I couldn't even imagine life without him.

The misty rain danced in the gentle breeze. Everything was shrouded with dampness. The haze hung in the air. Then, slowly, almost imperceptibly, the moisture settled everywhere in a blanket of dew.

I looked out my window and searched in vain for some patch of blue in the sky, even just a glimmer of sunlight would have been welcome. Grayness prevailed, the clouds absorbing all traces of light. *No such luck*, I thought. Today, March 20, 1955, was shaping up to be another typical Seattle day.

I let the drape slip out of my hand, and I turned from the window with a sigh. I thought about the last year with David. He was wonder-

Chapter One

ful—kind, funny, cute. Tonight I would be going out with him for his nineteenth birthday. I needed to get ready.

In view of the mirror, I turned to the right and to the left, critically analyzing the outside of Joan Franz.

"Well," I laughed, "not the most exciting profile in the world."

I stretched out my hand, picked up my hairbrush, and tried rearranging some stray strands of my dishwater-blond, bouncy curls. I caught my eye in the mirror and laughed. *Well, Joan, not much good a little ol' hairbrush will do.* I set the brush down. After a few seconds of critical assessment, I sighed and turned away from the mirror, thinking, *When you start with mediocre, you can't get much better than mediocre.*

I walked back to my bed and sat down. I thought about the change I had gone through the last year—Becoming part of David's life, growing more and more in love with him, and learning to know and love David's God.

The Lord Jesus Christ, what a name, what a Savior. I had never known the full extent of what Christ had done for me—stepping down from His throne in heaven to become a mere man; growing mature in a world that was full of sin and in need of the Savior; moving step by step, day by day, year by year in complete submission to His Father's will. Even when His Father's will pointed Him toward His own death, He went willingly.

I thought of the total commitment that was required and exemplified in Jesus Christ's sinless life, His total obedience to God. Who could possibly walk in His footsteps?

The church David had introduced me to preached about believers becoming like Christ. How was it possible? The idea of touching anything even close to the suffering Jesus Christ had experienced was beyond my comprehension. The total surrender and crucified self-will necessary for this Christlike commitment seemed so unattainable, out of the realm of human possibility.

I fell to my knees and prayed, suddenly overwhelmed with a need to surrender once again to God's ultimate plan. "Lord Jesus, make me like You. In my limited mind it doesn't seem possible, but I know, God, in Your Word it says that with You nothing is impossible. I believe in You, and I trust You to work in me to make me like You . . . whatever it takes. Thank you, my God, for hearing me and leading me. My life is in Your hands."

I felt the Holy Spirit move over me and through me, cleansing me and guiding me. I was overwhelmed with the goodness of Jesus.

I got up from my knees, confident of Christ's hand on my life and the evidence of His touch on my heart.

I walked back to the mirror to make the final touches necessary to be ready for my date with David. *Not that there is much to do*, I thought.

As I looked at my face, I noticed a difference. There was a radiance that came from within me. A gentle flush stained my cheeks, and my eyes were sparkling. A smile rested on my lipstick-free mouth. A laugh escaped my lips. "With prayer around, who needs makeup?"

The doorbell rang, and I jumped off my bed. Without another thought for my appearance, I grabbed my coat and purse and ran for the door. It had to be David, and I didn't want to keep him waiting. About halfway down the stairs I forced myself to slow. After all, my grandmother always said, "If you want to be treated like a lady, act like a lady." I chuckled at the memory.

When I got to the bottom of the stairs, I turned toward the door. David was there and he was talking to my dad. They were talking about—what else?—music.

David glanced up and saw me. Instantly his eyes lit up and a smile touched his lips. His gaze met and held mine. His blue eyes were full of soft light, with a hint of laughter and something else, something warm and caring. In his eyes, I felt beautiful and I smiled brightly. Across the room I could feel David's love radiating out to me.

"Hi," he quietly whispered.

My dad swung around.

"Oh, Joan, you're ready. I didn't hear you come down."

David closed the distance between us.

I looked into his eyes and stated, "Happy birthday, honey."

David hesitated at my words, slightly startled.

"Thank you, Joan. I almost forgot it was my birthday." He gave me a self-mocking, sideways smile.

Taking my coat out of my hands, he held it open for me. As my arms slipped into the sleeves, his hands brushed my shoulders. His touch hesitated with a gentle squeeze before his hands lifted.

"Ready?" David asked.

I nodded.

Chapter One

My dad, taking the hint, stepped toward the door. "You two have a nice evening and . . . don't do anything I wouldn't do." He laughed as I walked through the door with David close behind.

David reached down and took my hand. My hand felt natural in his, as if it belonged there. David's hand was warm and slightly rough, the hand of a man who worked hard—strong and dependable. Yet, as he laced his fingers with mine, the gentleness of his touch made me feel cherished as well as secure and safe.

"I was able to borrow Dad's car for tonight." David opened the passenger door as he continued, "What do you think about stopping to see the house I'm helping Dad build. It's going real well, and I'd like you to see it. We could drop in on the way to dinner."

"That sounds nice," I responded as I stepped inside the car, "I would like to see how it's coming along."

David broke out in a broad grin and, with a lilt in his voice, said, "Great!" He ran to the other side of the car, jumped in the driver's seat, and started the engine. David turned to look at me and smiled with a low chuckle. He lifted his eyes to mine and his jubilant mood was suddenly infused with a touch of seriousness.

Looking deep into my eyes he whispered, "I love you, Joan."

Even though it was not the first time he had said these words to me, my heart still beat faster. A shimmer of tears misted my eyes, and I breathed a soft, "I love you too, David."

His grin widened, and he raised his right forefinger to tap the end of my nose. David chuckled again, completely confident, and replied, "Then let's go."

As David pulled out of the driveway, I glanced out the window. The rain had stopped. The clouds were breaking up; the last sun rays of the day were managing to thread their way through the dissolving mist. It was a still, sweet twilight that seemed kissed with magic.

"How was school today?"

David's voice broke into my thoughts, and I turned toward him.

"Fine," I answered. "Although, as you know, choir is not the same without you there. Miss Charlton is having trouble finding someone to step into your shoes." I paused a few seconds and a frown formed on my face. "She doesn't say much to me. . . . I think she wants to discourage me from seeing you. I guess she thinks I'm a deterrent to your musical career."

Awakened

David leaned his head back and laughed. His amusement comforted me slightly, and I turned to face him. He quickly glanced in my direction, and I could see the merriment glinting in his eyes as he teasingly questioned, "And what do you think?"

His enjoyment of the conversation put me at ease; I started to play along with him.

"I think . . ."

I paused. Suddenly, I wanted to use the opportunity to get information from David, so, with determination, I continued, "I think you should tell me what you think."

David chuckled at my obvious ploy but willingly gave in.

"Well," he responded, "I already disappointed Miss Charlton when I went to work as a journeyman carpenter and rejected that music scholarship she was so keen on.

"I'm trusting Jesus to lead me into what He wants for my life, so don't worry too much about what Miss Charlton thinks. She has her own ideas for my life, and I have mine. I think I'll stick to mine. Besides," he laughed, "a voice like yours will inspire me for years to come." He glanced my way with a twinkle in his eye, ". . . And that's not only musically."

He turned back to the road, leaving me breathless. I heard his familiar chuckle floating in the air.

I didn't say anything for a few minutes. His words had started my heart racing. I let the full meaning of his words sink in. . . . *for years to come.* The idea of being with David for years overwhelmed me. I saw pictures of us laughing together, working together, being together. Children—our children—danced in my mind's eye, with David tossing them in the air, laughing.

"Joan," David's voice abruptly interrupted my fantasies, "we're here."

I looked out the car window and saw the house David was building with his father. David was coming around to open the car door. *Back to earth, Joan. . . . Slow down. Live for today, not for ten years from now.*

With that halfhearted rebuke in my mind, I stepped out of the car. David slipped his arm around my waist as he led me to the house.

I stepped inside. Even though the place had been swept clean, the unique fragrance of freshly cut wood lingered in the air. A couple of coveralls were piled on a table-saw in one corner. Some uncut studs lay stacked in the center of the room, ready for use. I gingerly stepped over the two-by-fours and followed David into the next room.

After observing the walls and layout of the room, I saw a beautiful wood chest sitting in a corner.

David moved toward the attractive box.

"Come over here, Joan, I want you to see this."

Contrasted against the rough lumber and drywall, the polished hardwood gleamed in the fading sunlight that shone through the window.

"I just finished this today," David excitedly explained. "What do you think?"

I looked at the shining luster of the wood. The design was beautiful. Each joint matched perfectly. My fingers itched to touch the smooth surface, to lift the lid and study the interior.

"Go ahead and take a look," David prompted. He hesitated, then spilled out the words, "It's a cedar chest, and it's yours. . . . I made it for you."

Midmotion I froze, stunned, as his words hit me.

"Oh, David—" I stammered.

"Come on, honey," David urged. "I want you to see all the compartments it has." His hand touched my elbow, gently encouraging my exploration.

I dropped to my knees and lifted the lid to examine the interior compartments. I was in awe at David's skill with wood.

"Look here." David squatted next to me, pointing at a row of silverware drawers along the side of the chest.

I opened the drawers one at a time, mesmerized by the beauty of David's craftsmanship.

"David . . ." I began.

"Yes?"

I opened the last drawer, and suddenly all words left my mouth. Tears sprang to my eyes, and I held my breath. A diamond ring sparkled in my eyes.

David's hand touched my shoulder. I could feel him kneeling next to me, his arm pulling me toward him. He leaned down, reaching out with his free hand, and gently lifted the small gold circle.

Still, I remained mute, overwhelmed at the sight of the delicate jewelry.

His touch came to rest on my elbow, where his gentle pressure helped me rise to my feet.

Awakened

"Will you marry me?" The soft, husky pitch of his voice vibrated through me, warm and caressing.

My eyes met David's. I saw David—my spiritual teacher, my friend, my love—and everything that he would become—my husband, my lover, my children's father. Present and future joined and became one within my heart, mingling together in a love that poured out of my eyes into his.

David caught his breath. He saw my love . . . and he felt it.

"I love you," I whispered, "and I've never wanted anything more in my life than to be your wife."

He let his breath out in one quick rush, and a smile blossomed on his handsome features. I thought I would never tire of watching that slow smile spread across his wonderfully strong face.

His fingers delicately held my left hand as he gently slipped the ring onto my finger. He brought my hand to his lips, sealing the band of promise with his kiss.

My heart soared. I loved David more than I thought was possible; more than anything I wanted to be his wife.

We stood eye to eye. The air shimmered with promise. There was a pause the length of a heartbeat while I looked into those wonderful, clear blue eyes, then his mouth touched mine.

"I've wanted to do that since the first moment I saw you this evening," he whispered against my lips. My arms slipped around his waist to hold him close.

"I love you more than you could ever imagine. I don't ever want to face the thought of being without you. I want to live with you for the rest of my life." His eyes glistened with sincerity and promise.

I touched his cheek with gentle fingers.

"I love you, David G. B. Anderson."

His smile blazed warm at my words.

He bent his head slightly so that his face was level with mine, and he once again kissed me lightly.

"Joan, I promise to always love you," he vowed. "I plan to love you forever and make you the happiest woman on earth."

I smiled at the seriousness of his declaration, my vision obscured with tears of joy.

"You've already made me the happiest woman on earth," I responded, gazing into his dear, sincere face.

Chapter One

David stared deeply into my eyes, serious and reverent, until suddenly he laughed.

"You said yes!" His words tumbled out in relief.

Stars invaded his eyes, and he pulled me into a tight embrace. I could hear the laughter rumbling in his chest. It was contagious, so I joined in.

The remainder of that night we walked on air. Secure in our love, we talked of our future as husband and wife. We felt enchanted, as if the world had stopped revolving to honor our love, and we were caught in a moment, as if time were suspended.

Soon after our engagement in the spring of 1955, my family scattered to live in different places. I graduated from high school in June and, in the same month, my older sister got married. Right after her wedding, my parents and younger siblings moved to Portland, where my father found a better job working in the design phase of fabric production. And, in the midst of this upheaval, I planned my wedding.

I was seventeen and just out of high school, so I didn't have much money for a big wedding. David's parents wanted a large celebration of family and friends for their son. So although they were not too enthusiastic about David getting married so young,

David and Joan's engagement portrait—March 1955

they generously offered to pay for the bulk of our expenses. David and I accepted their remarkable gift.

David was nineteen and, because he was under the age of twenty-one, he needed the signature of a legal guardian to authenticate the marriage license. David's mother signed this required document while successfully concealing her reluctance. David and I were so in love that we automatically assumed she was giving her blessing along with her signature.

Awakened

On August 12, 1955, David and I became husband and wife.

David and Joan's wedding—
August 12, 1955

We moved into a small room in the basement of Eric and Helen's home and, for the first couple of weeks, we lived in a state of newlywed bliss.

David and I quickly settled into a routine. David was in the School of Engineering at the University of Washington and, on the weekends, he served in the Naval Reserves. I worked in a typing pool at Seattle Hardware Company. David and I stayed to ourselves for the most part, but occasionally we left our basement apartment to visit David's parents upstairs.

Helen treated me quite nicely; she was a bit reserved, but I saw no sign of the domineering mother David had described. A calm, sedate atmosphere resided in their home.

About two weeks after we were married, I came home from work and, like usual, I entered through the upstairs front door, planning to take the inside stairway down to David's and my apartment. As I entered, I found my mother-in-law and our wedding photographer at the dining room table with the proofs from our wedding sprawled over the tabletop. I was thrilled and excited; I couldn't wait to see them.

"Oh, Joan," my mother-in-law remarked, "you're home." She smiled and waved her hands over the pictures.

"We were just sitting here looking at your wedding pictures. . . ." She paused. "I'm sure you don't mind."

David and Joan—1955

Without thinking, I blurted out a silly response I would have automatically delivered in the Franz home. I overacted with fake shock and said, "Oh, no! I can't believe you started without me!" Laughing, I continued my spoof, "I guess I'll just have to spank you."

Never dreaming my words would be offensive, I innocently ran out of the room with a parting comment, "I'll be right back to see the pic-

Chapter One

tures." I removed my coat and then joined the others to "ooh" and "ahh" over the portraits.

After the photographer left, I went downstairs to my apartment. Not a minute later, Helen burst into my room with a verbal tirade in full swing.

"I have never been so embarrassed in my life!" she screamed. "To think that you could say such a thing. You offended me in front of a complete stranger. Where is your respect? You ungrateful child, after all we have given you, to be treated like this. . . ."

I stood in the center of our living room, more shocked than I had ever been in my seventeen years of life. My jaw dropped at the site of this erupting volcano.

I cringed, wilting in the face of her anger.

The cruel words continued to spew from my mother-in-law's mouth. Her face contorted and her skin flushed. She was furious.

I tried to speak, wanting to apologize.

"Mom—" I began.

Without the slightest hesitation she continued out of control, "You deliberately set out to humiliate me."

"No—" I tried again.

"I never should have signed that marriage license. You are nothing but trouble."

"I'm sorry—" I said the words loud enough for her to hear.

She turned and left the room in a huff. I stood confused and trembling from the confrontation. I had never been subjected to so much hate. I was scared.

From that moment on, the relaxed, fun-loving home life to which I was accustomed was altered. My childlike, carefree manner of relating to others was not acceptable to Helen, and she made it clear to me. Consequently, I monitored every word I spoke.

I did everything I could to avoid conflict. I began entering our basement apartment through the back door. On occasion, I even went so far as to climb over a fence to gain access to the back door rather than risk being seen walking by her kitchen window.

Awakened

Innocent comments were blown way out of proportion. If I saw David across the backyard and addressed him with a teasing "Hi, stranger," I would be accused of trying to manipulate David by pressuring him to spend time with me instead of his parents.

If the bed was not made before I left for work in the morning, I would come home to accusations of "messy housekeeper" and "Can't you take care of my son?" The invasion of our privacy unnerved me.

I lived under Helen's thumb, and I felt the constant pressure. I could never let down my guard. But regardless of my vigil, I never seemed to do the right thing. My actions would unpredictably incite her, and then the yelling and crying would begin again, only to be followed by snide comments and rude looks.

Sometimes the intolerable tension would continue for months while I tried to figure out where I had erred. Sometimes I tried to hold out against the onslaught, not wanting to apologize for something I had not done. But, eventually, I would swallow my pride and ask for forgiveness just to stop the tension, even if it was only temporary. I was living near an active volcano, never knowing when the mountain would erupt but constantly aware of the potential for disaster.

Occasionally, I would share my feelings with David, but he was so accustomed to this kind of treatment that he was almost immune to my raw emotions. He felt bad, but he also didn't think there was anything that could be done. So I tried not to complain.

I did tell David that if I didn't love him as much as I did, I wouldn't be able to tolerate the situation. But I loved him too much to leave.

Besides the stabilizing force of David's love, the Lord Jesus became my anchor. Every day I asked God to help me, and every day He did. I began to take each day as it came and tried to be happy regardless of my circumstances.

At church they talked about being like Christ and to "fellowship in His sufferings." They also taught that, as Christians, we should aspire to be part of the church that is seen in Ephesians 5:27, ". . . a glorious church, not having spot or wrinkle or any such thing, but that she should be holy and without blemish." I was aware that I would have to face hardships to have the rough edges knocked off. First the cross, then the crown. To be like Jesus, I needed to be willing to take up my cross and follow Him.

Well, at this point in my limited experience, I assumed that my difficult family situation was the cross I would have to carry. I took it up

Chapter One

and, with Jesus' help, I was able to carry it. I knew that as I placed my burden on the altar of God, Jesus would "make the yoke easy and the burden light." And, of course, I knew that whatever the Lord allowed to touch my life would never be more than I could bear. In the Bible, God had promised to always "make the way of escape, that you may be able to bear it" (1 Cor. 10:13). I rested in that promise.

As each day went by, I walked on the beach of life with a relatively calm surf lapping at my toes. Then, occasionally, I felt the tug of the tide pulling at my feet, threatening to drag me into a dreadful ocean of despair. It was at those times that I clung to God's Word, trusting Him to keep His promise to help me bear my cross.

In my innocence, I didn't realize that God could allow a thundering wave of tragedy to roll over me and knock me off my feet, which would catch me in an undertow of emotional desperation. All my strength would be overwhelmed in the drowning surf, and all my own securities would be pounded into a reef.

I didn't know my world could fall apart and God would still not be breaking His promise.

Chapter Two

Ten years passed, during which time a foundation of memories formed. Each experience brought a new precious building block to the life we were creating together. The memory stones fell, one on top of the other, accumulating one by one.

- Moving into our own apartment and gaining some distance from David's parents.
- My personal experience of being baptized in the Holy Spirit.
- David's military service in the Navy, the Seabees.
- The birth of our first child; . . . then a miscarriage. . . . Later, the privilege of giving birth to a second daughter; . . . and two years later, a third, expanding our immediate family to five.
- David graduating from the University of Washington as a civil engineer.
- The formation of E & D Construction, a partnership between David and his father; . . . and the financial sacrifices necessary to build a viable construction business.
- David traveling to Brazil with Bernhard Johnson to lead a team of six young people to sing and preach for the summer months of 1964.

Awakened

Trip to Mt. Rainier—1956

The new parents with daughter Doreen—1958

Joan with Doreen and Donna—1961

Trio now complete with Doreen, Donna, and Susan—1963

Chapter Two

- Vacationing across the United States with our three young girls.
- David becoming more and more involved with work, designing and building apartment buildings; . . . building single-dwelling homes and selling them; . . . building churches . . .

The list could go on forever. It would flow with the memorable touches of time that molded us and fashioned our course. These circumstances touched us and shaped our lives. Every discouragement and every achievement was cemented together with laughter, tears, and love.

Gospel Team preparing for a trip to Brazil made the news in the Seattle *Post-Intelligencer*. David, on the far left, headed the six-member team—1964

Then, in September 1965, ten memory-filled years after David and I were married, David got sick. . . .

David and his dad were involved in constructing a church building in Redmond, Washington, and it was consuming all of David's time. Daytime was spent at the job site, and evenings were spent in his home office, laying out the next day's work plan or on the phone with his dad. But in mid-September, David began to experience flulike symptoms: headache, fatigue, body aches, somewhat loose stools, and slight nausea.

During this time Doreen was eight, Donna was five, and Susan was two and a half. Around September 12, two of our daughters came down with the flu—twenty-four hours of fever, diarrhea, and vomiting. So, David's condition a few days later was not at all surprising, especially considering the workaholic pace he was keeping.

At first, David ignored the slight pressure in his head, the pain in his joints, and the weariness associated with fighting a virus. He didn't even mention the symptoms to me. But his symptoms increased. A fever flared,

Awakened

and he ached all over. He was no longer able to hide his illness; he was utterly exhausted.

Still, David pushed through the symptoms, refusing to let the bug drag him down. He stubbornly clung to the belief that the infection would work its way out of his system whether he was in bed or not. He knew rest was a good idea, but he denied the fact it would accelerate his recovery.

As each day went by, David's illness worsened. The soreness in his muscles and joints was relentless; the fever continued. His temperature never dipped below 99 degrees, and was most consistently in the 100–101 degree range. A dizziness was also beginning to plague him. I noticed a dullness in his eyes that extinguished his normally bright gaze. He began moving slower than usual and occasionally reached for walls to steady himself.

Every morning, I tried to persuade David to stay in bed. . . .

"Listen, David, I know you feel you are indispensable, but you would be much more helpful at the job if you would just stay home and get over this flu." I paused slightly, then added some reasoning, "I'm sure your dad and the rest of the crew could manage without you for one day."

David was sitting on the edge of the bed, his face the color of putty, and he looked up at me. He could see the determination in my eyes, but he refused to admit I was right.

I tried to smother the feeling of futility as my frustration mounted.

"I know you mean well, Joan, but we are at a critical point on the church right now, and I've got to be there to show the crew exactly how to put the windows on the north side." He smiled slightly, trying to appease me.

His voice softened, and he conceded with, "I'll try to knock off a little early and come home." Then a sideways grimace briefly touched his mouth as he continued, "But, honey, I feel better if I get my mind off my aches and pains. On the job, I can push through the symptoms."

My shoulders sagged at his words, and I felt the weight of depression.

A rush of words flooded my mind, full of persuasive argument against his logic, but they stuck in my throat. I had been through this same scenario too many times already not to know the outcome of arguing with David. I swallowed my words.

I gave in to his stubbornness with a weary sigh.

Chapter Two

David moved slightly, straining to stand. He swayed unsteadily as he rose from the mattress. It was evident that his sickness was worsening.

David stumbled across the room to the bathroom, valiantly battling for each step yet trying to conceal his weakness. He fumbled with the light switch as he reached the small room.

I shook my head silently as I observed his struggle. I felt powerless to help him.

Every morning for a week and a half the drama would repeat itself, almost word for word. David would respond with "Don't worry, honey, I'll be OK. But, I can't rest until I . . ." Each day's answer varied only by the day's agenda. And David never came home early.

By the last week of September, David's condition had deteriorated even more. His appetite had vanished, and he was having loose stools two or three times a day. He was experiencing more nausea and sometimes vomited during the night.

Each day David expected to take a turn for the better. Instead, each day he got noticeably weaker.

By this time, I was getting very concerned. I was frustrated and angry because David wasn't slowing down and he wasn't taking care of himself. I continued to try to get him to take it easy—not an easy task, and up until now, impossible.

Each morning the tension mounted, increasing with my level of anxiety. David stubbornly refused to admit to his poor physical condition, and I was becoming more and more concerned.

The standoff did not last. David's body finally refused to obey his own mental commands.

The morning this happened, I got out of bed and grabbed my robe, slipping into my routine as easily as my arms slid down the sleeves of my bathrobe. I tiptoed across the carpeted floor, planning to go to the kitchen to start the coffee before waking David. As I made my way toward the bedroom door, David's heavy breathing captured my attention. I turned toward the bed, listening intently. David was breathing so hard it was like he had run a marathon and exhaustion was overwhelming him. His labored breath filled the stillness of the morning, urgently communicating David's utter weariness. As I turned back toward the doorway, a seed of panic was planted in my heart. I pushed it down, burying it deep as I made my way to the kitchen.

Awakened

On habit, I poked my head into the girls' room. I heard the slow, rhythmic breathing of their young bodies and I exhaled on a sigh filled with relief; at least *they* were healthy. I quietly closed the door behind me and went into the kitchen to start the coffee.

I breathed a short, desperate prayer, "God, help me to convince David to stay in bed today, please!" I felt a growing sense of urgency, and I felt helpless in my effort not to surrender to exasperation. My plea continued, "Jesus, You know how much he needs rest. Oh, God, please, . . . help me convince him to stay home!"

I finished the prayer with a quick "Thank you, Jesus" and made my way back to the bedroom. I walked through the door and braced myself for what had become our daily showdown. At the bedside, I leaned over David.

It hardly seemed possible, but David's breathing had become even more labored. The seed of panic I suppressed earlier began taking root.

I gently reached out to wake David, and I touched his shoulder. Immediately my hand drew back, my skin felt singed by the heat coming off his body. David was hot!

Slowly, David stirred. His eyelids lifted slightly, revealing glazed and scarcely focused eyes. Then they fell shut again as if the effort to open his eyes was too much for him. Moments later, after another try, David valiantly strained his gaze on me. He attempted a weak smile.

"Time to get up?" he whispered. His voice cracked as his breath left his lips with a soft groan, the effort of speaking costing him greatly.

I felt I was on the threshold of a belated and pointless victory. I realized the choice for getting up had finally been taken from David. There would be no argument today.

As I watched, he made a futile attempt to raise his head from the pillow. David rolled to his side and bent his elbow. Wrist flexed and palm down, he tried to push himself off the mattress. Immediately, the remaining color drained from his face and his arm collapsed. His youthful strength, once taken for granted, had been incinerated. His body was burning up with fever. Dizziness and nausea overwhelmed him, and he was forced to close his eyes as sweat broke out all over his body.

"Honey," he moaned. His voice broke, muffled by the blankets. Something that was meant to resemble a laugh escaped his parched lips. He ineffectively tried to moisten them, his tongue sticking to the dehydrated surface. His breath caught and held as he tried to summon the strength to communicate.

His hot breath seared my cheek as I leaned closer to hear David's words and, finally, he was able to announce, "I think I'll stay home today." He opened his eyes long enough to see if I had caught the irony of his joke. And then, all fight gone, his eyelids finally surrendered to the need for rest.

I left David to sleep and returned to the kitchen. I picked up the phone and called our medical provider. A nurse heard my story and told me to keep David in bed, and to give him aspirin and plenty of liquids. "He needs rest," she said. Then she concluded our conversation with, "If he is not better in two or three days, you will need to bring him in to see a doctor."

I breathed deep, said, "OK," and hung up the phone. I followed the nurse's instructions.

David missed two days of work, but his condition continued to deteriorate. He was no longer having diarrhea, but he continued to vomit intermittently. His temperature remained in the 101–102 degree range, and his dizziness never let up. The room revolved around him whether he sat or laid down; his stomach swayed with the motion.

The seed of panic grew in my mind.

"David," I said. It had been two days since my conversation with the nurse, so I went to him to see if he would be willing to see a doctor.

David's eyes fluttered open. I met his bewildered look, smiling to cover my apprehension and to reassure him.

"Huh, . . . what?" he croaked through parched lips.

"It's just that I need to know if you . . ." I started to ask.

David's eyes immediately bulged, and he rolled onto his side, halting my question.

"The bathroom—" he insisted.

His hands flew to his head to grip his throbbing skull. His mouth clamped shut, holding back the nausea. Sweat glistened on his face and arms as he strained to stand, his muscles vibrating with exertion. I grabbed his arm as he struggled for balance.

Just in time, he dropped to his knees in front of the toilet and retched. Perspiration ran down his face and dripped onto the toilet seat. His arms shook as they tried to hold his upper body away from the bowl.

Awakened

The sound of David heaving again spurred me into action. I turned the faucet on, running the cool water to lukewarm. Soaking a washcloth, I turned to see David starting to rise from the floor. While gently washing his face, he leaned against me, and I almost staggered under his weight.

"Let's get you in bed again, OK?" I suggested.

David merely blinked his glazed eyes in affirmation.

Awkwardly, we stumbled back to the bed. Once under the sheets, David's eyelids immediately began to droop.

I stood next to the bed and watched him fall into a deep, fever-induced sleep. My question of what to do next had been eclipsed by David's unavoidable trip to the bathroom.

Slowly and quietly, trying not to disturb David, I left the room and made my way toward the kitchen once again.

What should I do? I thought. I was accustomed to letting David make the decisions.

My first thought was to call the doctor. But David hated going to the doctor. He had always had an aversion to hospitals, and he was especially reluctant about going to our medical carrier. We belonged to a co-op of sorts in which a large group of doctors shared patients. This meant that whenever a person needed medical attention, they saw whichever physician happened to be on call. David hated this impersonal policy, so we used the service as little as possible. Moreover, David said he preferred to leave his health in God's hands.

My next option was to call my mother-in-law. I swallowed my reluctance and reasoned with myself: She was a nurse and she was David's mother. I reached for the phone and picked up the receiver. Placing my finger in the rotary dial, my hand stopped.

I had plenty of experience to justify my caution. Even after we moved into our own place, she still wanted to control our lives, and I still had to carefully screen everything I said to her. But I needed help.

My fingers moved, dialing the number.

Helen answered. She expressed her growing concern about David and her belief that he needed medical attention. She offered to call their family doctor, Dr. Lehmann.

I willingly gave her the go-ahead.

Later, she called me back with the news that her doctor couldn't do anything for David. Dr. Lehmann didn't belong to our medical group.

Chapter Two

I thanked my mother-in-law for trying. Then, before I hung up, I promised her that I would call our co-op again and get an appointment.

I reached for the telephone once again and called our medical carrier. I explained to the office staff what was happening to David, and I was referred to a nurse. Again, I explained the situation and the nurse's response was frustrating, yet expected. "You will have to bring him into the office for the doctor to make a diagnosis." I questioned the nurse about whether it was wise for David to go outside. She responded with, "You have no choice. If you want a doctor to see him, he must come into the office."

I made the appointment. I brought the girls to my mother-in-law's and asked her to baby-sit while I took David to the doctor. Pleased that David was going to get medical attention, she agreed.

It was all I could do to get David out of bed and dress him. He complained about the dizziness in his head and would grab his skull and moan. Then he would end up in the bathroom to relieve his nausea. But, finally, I managed to get David out to the car and to the doctor's office.

Unfortunately, when we got there, we were confronted with the standard administrative maze: paperwork, waiting, red tape, waiting, questions and more questions, waiting and more waiting . . .

I looked into David's glazed, fever-burned eyes. He let his lids drop closed. His appearance vacillated, one moment his cheeks were flushed with fever, and the next minute he would pale and blanch as pain pierced through his skull. His features pinched together and lines fanned around his eyes; then they would soften and relax as the pain eased, replaced with dots of sweat from the persistent fever.

His eyelids opened again. Dryly, he croaked, "I'll be OK, honey. Don't worry."

A slight half-smile momentarily touched his chapped lips as he continued, "I'm sure the doc will help." He moved his hand, gesturing to the other occupants in the room, "He must be worth waiting for." His lips twitched ever so slightly in appreciation of his own sarcasm, and his humor offered a moment of entertainment in the boredom.

Eventually, we did get to see David's "doc."

"David probably has an unspecific viral infection," the doctor matter-of-factly stated.

The doctor turned to me, his eyes never quite meeting mine. He reiterated the familiar instructions on what I should do for David.

"Put him in bed, give him plenty of liquids, and have him take two aspirin every four hours."

I tried to feel relieved by the doctor's nonchalance, but a nagging doubt plagued me.

I glanced over at David before turning back to the doctor. What I saw pushed me beyond my usual shyness.

"Are you sure he will be all right?" I pointed to David. "Isn't there something else you can do?" My voice held a slight hint of begging, but I didn't care.

"As you already explained, a lot of his problem has to do with the fact that he wouldn't slow down. It will just take time, plenty of rest and lots of fluids," he paused, thinking. "I'll give David a prescription for sulfadiazine. This is an antibacterial agent that will kill any possible bacteria that might be causing his symptoms, but it might not do anything. If his body is fighting a virus, this drug won't help."

I swallowed any more of my anxious questions, convincing myself I was overreacting. My doubt seemed insignificant in light of his expertise and experience.

"OK," I said.

I went to David and took his arm, slowly leading him back to the car and home.

I followed the physician's instructions to the letter. I gave David the sulfadiazine and the aspirin. I tried to get as many liquids into him as possible. And he stayed in bed.

David was so sick, so nauseated, that anything he ate or drank kept coming back up. The medicine and the fluids were going in his mouth, but they were not staying in his body long enough to help him.

I was becoming frantic. There was no change in David's condition except that he seemed to be getting worse. From one minute to the next he alternated from being ghostly pale with icy shivers to being flushed and dripping with sweat. He tried valiantly to stay lucid and in good spirits, but the high fever sucked away all his energy, leaving him listless and uncommunicative.

Chapter Two

My energetic, happy, healthy husband had disappeared. His fever stayed high, and the dizziness relentlessly debilitated him. Every day seemed an eternity; each breath taken by David was a struggle. Repeated trips to the toilet relieved his incessant nausea. No food, water, or medicine could stand against the relentless and monstrous fever.

It was now the beginning of October. David had been sick for over two weeks, and I was praying for some letup in the ever-increasing illness.

I felt David's scorching breath as I leaned closer to him. I brushed a few strands of damp hair from his sweaty brow. My fingertips felt scalded by the burning fever. *Would it ever break?*

David stirred. His eyes opened slightly.

"Joan . . ." he rasped. He swallowed, trying to continue. "My head hurts. It feels like its going to bust open from the pressure. . . . And my neck, I can't move it too well."

My heart went out to him. I wanted to relieve his discomfort, but I didn't know how. Suddenly, he started shaking as feverish chills completely took over his body. His muscles twitched, and his teeth began to chatter. I moved my hand across his forehead and down his cheek. He was so hot—maybe even hotter than before. I swallowed, then breathed.

Think! my mind cried.

I took David's temperature. His eyelids lifted ever so briefly as I placed the mercury stick in his mouth, and then they drooped closed again. He tried to hold the thermometer in place with his lips, but his shivering made the small task exhausting.

"It's OK," I soothed. My hand held the thermometer under his quivering tongue as well as I could with his teeth occasionally banging against the glass. I prayed for an accurate reading. With trembling fingers, I removed the thermometer. The instrument turned over in my hand, and I strained to read the mercury. I blinked my eyes. The silver line stopped just over 104 degrees. David was burning up!

I looked at David with moist eyes, my throat aching with unvoiced dread. I swallowed slowly. *Stop overreacting, Joan,* I admonished myself. *It's just a fever,* I continued, trying to calm myself. *Sure, it may be just a fever, but it has lasted way too long. And 104 degrees is much too high.*

By now, I had lost all confidence in the doctor's diagnosis. The medication was doing nothing, maybe even making David worse. My growing uneasiness drove me to bundle up David again and take him back to the doctor.

By the time we got to the doctor's office, David could hardly walk. He was burning up, shaking with chills, and I had to half-carry him into the exam room. Again, after the unreasonable wait, the doctor came in. Amazingly, it was the same man who had seen David before. I could hardly believe our good fortune. The physician took a brief look at David, glanced at me, and motioned for me to meet him outside the room. I quickly stepped through the doorway. The doctor was close behind.

"What do you want me to do?" the doctor's angry question slammed into my ears as soon as the door clicked shut.

I looked at him in stunned disbelief. His words completely destroyed my expectations and my hopes. A heaviness came over me. Mutely, I stared at the doctor. He continued to scrutinize me as if I were an unwanted problem he wasn't quite sure how to be rid of. The oppressive silence hung in the air.

Finally, after countless, unnerving seconds, I meekly answered the aggravated doctor. "Help him," I stuttered.

The doctor rocked on his feet, leaned toward me, and emphatically spit out his rebuttal.

"I already told you what to do." His eyes dropped from my face in midsentence, as if I were not worthy of his precious time. His feet shifted back and forth, his pent-up energy driving his frustration.

Astonished, I stared at him, not quite believing what I heard. He brushed his hand through his hair and muttered to himself. After a weary sigh, he finally returned his attention to me.

"It is just going to take time," he emphasized each syllable, talking to me as if I were a small, errant child. His mouth snapped shut as his last syllable hung in the air between us.

He started to turn away, his last word echoing in my mind: *time* . . .

The doctor's dismissal provoked me to respond.

"But, Doctor," I stopped his retreat with my hand on his arm. "How much time? David is so sick."

He turned back to me with a condescending, withering look meant to silence me. But motivated by genuine concern, I continued.

"David hasn't kept any food or liquid down for several days. He can't seem to shake this fever. In fact, his temperature has gone up to

104 degrees." I kept going, refusing to let up. "Did you really look at him in there?" I pointed toward the room the doctor and I had just left.

"OK," the doctor obliged. "We'll stop the sulfadiazine and see what happens."

I was stunned.

"Isn't there anything else you can do for him?" I boldly pleaded with the doctor.

For the first time the doctor really looked at me.

"Well," he sneered, "if I had a choice, I would give him a wife that would understand plain English when told he needs to rest, and not a woman who continually drags him out of his sick bed to come bothering his doctor all the time."

He turned around and haughtily walked away.

I stared after him, dumbfounded. I was shocked and wounded by his words. His accusation was a sting of doubt in my mind, *Was I really hurting David?* The doctor's venomous words painfully released their poison. I stood immobilized, paralyzed by my doubt and fear.

I'm not sure how long I stood there, distraught and shocked beyond belief, but I finally shook myself and forced my feet to move.

By the time David and I got home, I was beside myself. I felt like I was in a cold fog, looking for a door that would lead to warmth and shelter but finding none. I was in a dark, senseless place. God seemed far away, and people, especially doctors, seemed completely unreliable and untrustworthy. Where could I go for help? I could feel anger and frustration getting the best of me. I didn't know what to do.

I began to see David's illness as a great menacing monster, lying in wait in the dark to completely devour us—a monster with no face, no name, and a monster against which neither David nor I could defend ourselves. I felt helpless and out of control. Something had to be done about David because he was getting worse, not better. But I wasn't sure what.

There was no one to turn to but God. Helpless, I prayed, "Lord, help me! Show me what to do. I am powerless and afraid. I need you to take care of David. I give up." My words seemed empty and hollow, bouncing back at me, but at least they were said.

Over the weekend, I watched David worsen. His fever persisted. Severe, pounding headaches continued, and even the slightest motion near him intensified the spinning in his head.

Helen was also worried about David. She was convinced he was not getting proper care. On this point, we were in full agreement. So she grabbed the reins. On Monday morning, she called their own physician again and convinced him that we needed his help. Reluctantly, Dr. Lehmann said he would come take a look at David that evening. On October 11, 1965, Dr. Lehmann made a house call.

Dr. Lehmann was a kind, gentle man in his midforties. He was a tall, Jewish man with dark hair and sharp, foreboding features that often led to an incorrect first impression. Contrary to his outward demeanor, he met me with a confident handshake and a warm, fatherly smile. His presence quickly put me at ease, which was an incredible accomplishment after what had transpired with the other doctor.

Dr. Lehmann examined David, and, with a slight frown, he read David's temperature and counted his pulse. He looked into David's ears, down his throat, and studied his eyes. His hands gently massaged David's neck, feeling for swelling. He had David sit up so he could analyze David's heart and lungs. The frown on the doctor's face deepened in concentration as he listened to David breathe in and out. Slowly, the doctor closed his eyes and blinked them open again. He pondered the evidence before him, straining for a diagnosis.

The doctor cleared his throat and swallowed, stalling for time.

Abruptly penetrating the silence of the room, Helen's voice intruded, "What is your impression, Doctor?" she pressed.

Dr. Lehmann's head immediately popped up, his gaze finding Helen. "I've checked him over, but I don't see any obvious cause for his condition. He is dehydrated from the fever and lack of fluid retention. He is a very sick young man. You have reason to be concerned; there is definitely something wrong. . . . I'm just not sure what."

He glanced at me, then looked back at my in-laws. His hand cupped his chin then slid over his cheek. His fingers slowly drifted backward, through his hair and down his neck. Stopping there, his fingers began to massage the building tension in his muscles. His head dipped and his brow creased in concentration. Under his breath, I heard Dr. Lehmann whisper, "I wonder?"

Chapter Two

He cleared his throat and straightened.

"How do you feel about admitting him into Ballard Hospital for some further tests. There are several possibilities that come to mind, but I need more information."

"What do you think, Doctor?" Helen persisted.

"Well . . . infectious mononucleosis is an outside possibility. David has some swelling of his lymph nodes, and his acute fever could probably be explained by this type of disease. The problem is that a good percentage of the time, infectious mono is accompanied by lesions of the mouth and throat. David does not have those. But, on the other hand, he does complain of a slightly sore throat. Another conceivable explanation is labyrinthitis, an inflammation of the internal ear. This could explain the dizziness accompanying the fever. I just can't say for sure what the problem is without running some definitive tests."

The doctor paused, weighing the wisdom of being involved with another doctor's patient. After a brief hesitation, he continued, "I could admit him into Ballard Hospital for some tests; but, to do that, I need your permission."

He turned his head to look at me. "It's your decision."

I could sense Dr. Lehmann's caution. He was being careful about saying or doing too much for us because we were members of a medical group to which he did not belong. I realized that he needed my complete authorization to treat David. I was so disgusted with the lack of help I had received from our health carrier that I needed no further prompting. Immediately I said, "Yes, please, do something . . . anything."

After a quick phone call asking my sister to come watch the girls, we got ready to go to Ballard Hospital.

Once we entered the hospital, David's mother took control. She rushed around getting the hospital staff to do everything they could for David. I walked slightly behind the bustling crowd as they ushered David toward his room. I felt like I was in a bad dream. It scared me. I blinked, then I blinked again, trying to clear the fog in my mind. Time stood still. Sounds buzzed in my ear. David's parents talked to people and signed papers. I stood numb. Then, finally, David was admitted into Ballard Hospital with a preliminary diagnosis of acute mononucleosis.

Dr. Lehmann gave David a shot of penicillin and had him swallow a few pills of Tigan. Then the hospital staff took David to run initial tests.

Awakened

Dr. Lehmann informed us they wouldn't have the results until the next morning. I stared blankly at him.

My mind registered some rustling going on to the side of me, and I turned to see what was going on. David's mom was reaching for her coat and slipping it on. This relatively mundane activity slowly registered on my mind, and I realized that perhaps nothing more could be done for David at this time.

I glanced back at Dr. Lehmann, and he gave me a kind smile. I remembered the explosion of ridicule from the previous doctor in response to any question but I tentatively returned his smile and meekly asked, "Is there nothing more you can do for David tonight?"

Dr. Lehmann smiled again with kindness and sympathy and opened his mouth to speak.

"Now, Joan—" David's mom intruded, her words preempting the doctor's response, "the doctor is doing everything he can. He'll watch and make sure everything is OK." She turned to Dr. Lehmann with a sugary smile, "Isn't that right, Doctor." Without pausing, she continued, never allowing the doctor a chance to answer. "Why don't you come home with us and, if anything happens, he will let us know." She reached for my coat and placed her arm behind me.

"Come along, dear." She nudged me from behind with a gentle push toward the door.

I stiffened. My feet were planted. I knew I did not want to leave David right at that moment. I turned to my mother-in-law and said, "No, I'm going to stay here for awhile."

She sighed, unexpectedly relenting.

"OK, dear, whatever you want." A sticky-sweet smile accompanied her words. "Give us a call when you are ready to come home and Eric will come get you."

I nodded silently.

The fact that David and I didn't own a car came crashing in on me. We did not own one because every spare penny went back into David and Eric's business, E & D Construction. We had never really needed a vehicle anyway because David's parents were generous, letting us use theirs. But now, with David incapacitated, I felt as though I was suffocating, smothered by charity. I wanted to fight against the robbery of my personal freedom. My independence was dependent on David. I felt helpless, completely incapable of stopping this thievery.

Chapter Two

I stood and waited, watching David's parents go out the door toward their car and home. As the steel doors swung shut, I turned and headed for David's room.

I moved through the hallways. My senses were assaulted by the sanitized smell of sickness, and my stomach flopped. I was scared. The realization hit me: *David is so sick that he needs to be hospitalized!*

The monster was closing in on us. It was advancing, no longer just waiting and lurking in the shadows. I could feel its hot breath on my neck. It was stomping on our comfortable little world and shattering it.

God . . . help us! my mind cried. I closed my eyes and breathed deep, trying to bury the panic. I talked to myself, *Calm down, Joan, David is in good hands. . . .*

As I opened the door to David's room I was greeted with a weak, "Hi, honey."

"Hi," I said as I walked toward the bed and sat on the edge. His voice, though weak, soothed my tattered nerves. His love and acceptance of me bolstered me, and I was able to inquire, "How were the tests?"

"They took some blood and urine. They'll do more tests tomorrow." He swallowed and continued. "Most of the results are not back yet, but I do know they ruled out the inner-ear thing, the labyrin- something."

"Are they going to test for the infectious mono tomorrow?" I asked.

"Yeah, that's what Dr. Lehmann said."

"Good," I encouraged.

I looked at David's face, he looked utterly weary.

"How are you holding up?"

David turned his head and looked at me seriously. "I really don't know," he said. "I feel so groggy, and I'm having trouble thinking clearly, and . . . and I am so hot."

I touched his hand lying on the bed. He felt very warm, but at least he was now in a hospital bed with help on every side.

I breathed deep, sighing in weary relief. The burden of David's welfare was lifting with each breath I took.

I brought David's hand to my lips and kissed the hot, dry skin.

His eyes drifted shut as he murmured contentedly, "Thanks, . . . I needed that."

I smiled, happy to be with this wonderful man.

I stayed with David until visiting hours were over. As I stood to leave, I quietly asked if he wanted me to bring anything from home. His

Awakened

eyes met mine, and I caught a glimpse of my husband's familiar twinkle as he replied, "Yeah, I would love to have my own pillow."

He moved slightly, gesturing to the pillow under his head as he continued. "This hospital lump-of-stuffing is more like a rock than a pillow."

A fragile laugh escaped my lips as I bent to give David a kiss goodbye. My heart felt lighter knowing he had not lost his sense of humor, even as sick as he was.

My steps had a slight buoyancy to them as I made my way toward the hospital exit. The rest of the evening was free of immediate worries or fears. I was confident I was leaving David with the best medical care available. Someone was actually going to look after him; someone believed he needed care and was willing to give it.

The monster was still out there, but I could no longer feel it breathing down my neck. The retreat of this menacing presence made it possible for me to relax a little and breathe deeply of the night air as I walked to the car where Eric was waiting for me. I actually smiled as I remembered David's humorous parting words.

Little did I know that those words would be the last conversation I would have with the "David" I had grown to love.

Chapter Three

The next day was Tuesday, October 12. I brought David's pillow up to my chest as I stopped and glanced down the corridor of the hospital. I was alone. Relieved by the sight of the empty hallway, I sighed. I wasn't in the mood to deal with any communication, even simple eye contact.

The sounds of hospital life touched my ears as I continued down the hall. The soft beeping of monitors and the squeaking of bed frames surrounded me. The smells of sterility mingled with other scents undefined yet undeniably associated with sickness—an unnerving reminder of our human frailty. I moved quickly down the hall, trying to escape the unique hospital odor.

My mind focused on my mission. I pressed the pillow closer, and David's scent drifted into my nostrils from the pillowcase. His distinct aroma brought a picture of him to mind. He felt so near, almost as if I were holding him in my arms.

As I glanced down at the soft cushion, my mind flashed to moments with David and his warm, loving touch. *Well, it's not exactly like holding David*, my mind refuted, and a slight smile touched my lips. I was comforted by the thought I would soon be with him.

I quickened my pace through the hospital. I couldn't wait to see him; it seemed forever since I had left him last night. I needed to see him, to be with him, to touch him. I needed to see if he had made any progress.

David's parents and his aunt and uncle had been with him during the morning. I had anxiously waited for their return with the car so I could be with him myself. The memory of the pity in their eyes resurfaced in my mind as I passed the vacant nurse's station. Their words burned in my ears: "We're sorry, Joan. We're praying for David."

I clung to the image of David valiantly smiling through his pain to offset their well-meaning but depressing condolences. When I reached David's room, I quietly opened the door and stepped inside. Lowering David's pillow, I walked toward the bed as the door clicked shut.

He moved restlessly, but I didn't think anything of it. I chalked it up to being in an unfamiliar bed. Anyway, who wouldn't be uncomfortable after being sick for so many days. How long had it been, two weeks? No, three weeks! Time had seemed to whip around me like a hurricane; the days blended together in a blur. Moments of David panting with fatigue, and burning with hell-fired fever, continually battered my mind, threatening to overshadow my recollection of a strong, wise, and loving man.

I breathed deep, and slowly released the air from my lungs. I tried to recall the relief I had felt the night before when I realized that David was finally getting medical attention. *At least he has someone qualified to watch over him. Someone is trying to find out why David is not getting well.* The thought calmed me, and my glance swept toward the figure on the bed.

David moved, twitching slightly, somewhat erratic. His eyes were closed, pinched tight with tension, almost as if he were experiencing a bad dream. His face was flushed and clammy with perspiration. Drops of sweat glistened on his forehead, his honey-brown hair disheveled.

"Hi, honey, I brought your pillow from home."

David did not respond. I noticed his bedclothes were wrinkled and in disarray; skewed around the bed frame with little regard for tidiness.

"How are you feeling?"

Again, no response. That was not like David.

"David? . . . " I walked to the bed.

Immediately, David beat his legs and flailed his arms against the mattress. Squirming and wriggling, he thrashed about. His writhing further tangled the sheets.

What is going on? my mind questioned uneasily. *Is this a joke?*

Chapter Three

David moved his head in my direction, and a low garbled moan escaped his lips. I caught his eye for a split second, expecting some sort of response or recognition. There was none. His vacant stare stabbed me. Clearly, this wasn't a joke. David didn't know I was there. He was mumbling to himself, his eyes darting around the room, piercing everything but seeing nothing. He babbled louder, incessant droning that said nothing. The inane clatter splattered around the room and bounced off the walls.

I looked around the room and back at David, praying that this nightmare was only an illusion and David would reach out for the pillow I still held limply in my arms.

I blinked, trying to clear away the sight of my disoriented husband. *This can't be real.* The numbness of denial descended over me.

"David," I mouthed the words with my gaze unfocused, "the girls say they love you and are waiting for you to come home. . . ." My words petered out, and I didn't know how to continue. I sucked in my breath and held it. Trying to concentrate, I prayed for some kind of response from David.

Suddenly, an abrupt groan demanded my attention. David's body jerked, jumping off the mattress and bouncing back as if jolted by a surge of electricity. Shocked, my eyes flew to his face. More incoherent mumbling and muttering pushed through his tense, gritted teeth. Straining against an imaginary foe, David continued to shove his body around in a frenzied propulsion, pulled by some monster in his mind.

My fright grew. I tried to push it down, telling myself I was getting worked up over nothing. Then David's incoherent jabber penetrated my thoughts, and fear engulfed me. My physical and emotional resources were exhausted, and I was walking a thin tightrope of sanity.

My breathing grew shallow, short hiccups of air barely touched my lungs. I felt dizzy.

What is happening to David? my mind screamed. Something was definitely wrong—but what?

Consumed with dread, I stepped backward. Was this really occurring or was this possibly a nightmare? *Where is everyone . . . the doctors . . . the nurses?*

My hands began to sweat. My clammy fingers felt for the doorknob. My stomach felt queasy. My legs trembled. I needed air. I was suffocating with panic. *This is wrong—No!* My mind refused to accept the evidence

Awakened

before my eyes. Absolutely no way was this real. God wouldn't let this happen to me . . . to David. This seemed too close to hell. My body felt like a throbbing, exposed nerve—I had to shut down.

I stood outside David's room, my eyes darting back and forth from one object to another in the corridor, desperately trying to find something familiar and safe. I slowly became aware of the loud, uneven rhythm of my heart, its broken cadence carrying surges of adrenaline through my system. I closed my eyes, breathing deep to quell the rising hysteria. *You're dreaming* came the only conscious thought—the safeguard of my sanity.

As my heartbeat slowly returned to some semblance of normalcy, I opened my eyes, hoping to wake up on the couch back at home. My eyes focused on the sterile hospital ward. I wasn't dreaming—this terror was real.

I have to tell someone. The single thought slammed through my mind.

Moving away from David's door, I stumbled and almost fell, recovered, then turned and raced toward the nurses' station. I found myself face to face with a nurse. She looked up from the chart she was reading, her expression reflecting well-practiced sympathy.

I wanted to yell and scream, *What have you done to my husband!* Instead, I stood there, speechless, my tongue swollen with stifled anguish. I swallowed and forced myself to speak.

"Excuse me. . . ." I kept pressing my voice, praying that I could communicate my concern to the nurse without losing my fragile control. "Can you tell me what is wrong with David?"

When faced with my question, the nurse's façade shattered. Her chin dropped, and she stared at me dumbfounded. Without caution, she responded to me in her surprise, rapidly shooting a question in return. "Didn't anyone tell you what happened?"

My apprehension intensified at her words, and I choked out a forced "No." My fragile hold on my emotions failed, and I started to cry. I felt the wetness begin to cascade over my cheeks, and I was helpless to stop the flow.

The nurse stepped from behind the counter. Her arm went around me and, with gentle pressure, she led me to the waiting area. There, she finally addressed my question, this time with reserve and deliberation—just the facts, no emotion, no drama.

Chapter Three

I reined in my emotions, shutting them off as best I could, trying to regain some semblance of control to hear what the nurse had to say.

"I'm sorry, Mrs. Anderson, but it appears that between five and seven o'clock this morning, David became delirious."

I sat there, staring at her. I was in shock and unable to respond.

The nurse saw tears slowly make their way over my cheeks to my chin, then drop unceremoniously onto my clasped hands. When she continued speaking, she tried to explain in more detail why David was totally unresponsive.

"The delirium is due to the extended time David's temperature has been too high," she recited.

My mind was in a fog that robbed me of any sense of time or place. *Delirium* . . . It didn't make sense. I didn't understand. I didn't *need* to understand—I just wanted my husband back.

I shuddered. The apprehension, confusion, and fear I was experiencing had escalated to such a degree that the emotional pressure was making me tremble. But it wasn't until I saw the nurse glance down at my clenched hands that I became aware of my shaking.

She awkwardly tried to reassure me by placing her arm around me again. I felt the warmth of her human touch, but it was not enough to stop my trembling.

Disoriented, I closed my eyes and took a deep breath in an instinctive attempt to clear my thoughts. My eyelids twitched, my efforts to focus in vain.

Jesus, help me, I breathed. The urgent whisper escaped my lips without sound. I shivered. My cry penetrated heaven, and my fragile faith began to create a cover of protection to buffer me from my own emotions. I drew another calming breath and opened my eyes. I looked down at my hands; they were beginning to sting from the digging impact of my fingernails. I moved my hand to finger the small indentations, automatically soothing the soreness. A focused question formed in my mind and loosened my tongue.

"Will you please explain this to me?" I asked. I was ready to try to understand.

The nurse answered, "Delirium is what happens to a person when their mind is exposed to severe or prolonged trauma. In David's case, we assume the trauma would be his high fever."

I continued, "Why is he acting the way he is?"

"When a person is delirious, he is mentally disturbed. The mind can no longer function in a normal manner. The result is disorientation, confusion, jumbled speech, and sometimes even hallucinations," she defined.

"But," I tried to understand, "David is physically out of control. He is flinging his body around the bed. Is this frenzy normal? What does that have to do with his mind?"

The nurse responded to my frankness.

"We don't know. Right now the doctors think David is in pain. He is confused and disoriented, and he answers questions inappropriately; so he is difficult to evaluate because we can't get any intelligent responses from him. We just don't have any concrete answers."

I let her words sink in. Weakly, I pushed for more information.

"What is being done for David right now?" I inquired.

"The doctors are planning to run some more tests," she answered. Then, trying to reassure me, she continued, "Your husband has excellent doctors and they are doing all they can for him."

I nodded.

I couldn't think of any other questions, so I sat quietly, trying to absorb everything the nurse had told me. Knowing there was nothing else she could say, the nurse quietly left the room, leaving me alone with my thoughts.

The underlying message penetrated deep into my soul. I understood. David was sinking deeper and deeper into an unknown quicksand, and no one seemed able to reach him. The monstrous illness was in control of David.

I looked head-on into the jaws of this preying "monster." It was hungry and closing in fast. I clearly saw the misery and heartache ready to overtake us. The grief tormented me. *Where was God? Could I really trust Him?* My feeble faith faltered; my protective shield slipped. The hopelessness of the situation overwhelmed me. I had never felt so alone in my life. I sat in the waiting area, just staring straight ahead.

Time stood still.

My feelings epitomized the worst nightmare: I felt totally at the mercy of something malevolent and evil. This was a horrendous thunderstorm out of control. I felt powerless. For the first time, I felt real fear of what the future might hold—the horrid thought of *What if David dies?* pierced through my brain. The storm raged. A real conflict began in my soul.

Chapter Three

I believed if I lived right, God would protect me and make all the circumstances in my world good—and possibly a bit of wonderful thrown in for proper behavior.

Now reality glared at me, forcing me to come face to face with the realization that my commitment to Christ was not necessarily a guarantee of life treating me kindly. My rosy view of life was crumbling around me, and I was not prepared. I felt strange—almost betrayed.

I tried to pray, but my mind refused to function. I couldn't form coherent thoughts or put my feelings into any kind of order. The only thought I could recognize screamed from my heart through silent lips: *Why?* The single demanding question blazed around in my head, scorching my soul and searing my spirit. I was consumed with grief and doubt. My tormented cry left my heart and flew toward the silent heavens.

I was afraid. I could feel my faith in God ready to snap. My human reasoning couldn't come up with any logical answers for my situation. Was I really completely at the mercy or the whim of evil? Questions flooded my mind: *Could God be in full control of our lives and still let this happen to us? Was it possible for this horror to actually be allowed by a loving Heavenly Father? Did God really allow this kind of pain and disappointment?*

I had no answers.

Everything I believed in, everything I had been taught, pointed to God's sovereignty. I had believed in His absolute authority and that He had dominion over everything on earth and in heaven. *But that means God is allowing this nightmare to create havoc in our lives—God is letting it happen.*

The thought nauseated me.

Then a bitter question shot through my mind: *Would God actually let David die?* Dark despair overwhelmed me. The essence of my belief in a loving God who protects His children was being shaken to the very core. Silently, I stood. I cried.

Then I remembered the scripture, "He . . . sends rain on the just and on the unjust" (Matt. 5:45). I had seen those words and read them many times. I had thought I understood them. But never in my wildest imagination had I expected the rain to drown me in a flooding torrent.

Grasping for a lifeline, I asked God for understanding.

"Lord," I honestly prayed, "I'm confused. I don't know what to believe anymore. Help me . . ." My petition petered out as I took a breath. My lips trembled as I tried to control the raging storm in my soul. "Oh,

God, are You even here?" I hesitated. My faith was so weak. Then my words tumbled over my lips in desperation.

"Lord, I want to believe in You. I can't go through this without You, but I'm having trouble. I don't understand why this is happening—why You let it happen. It just doesn't seem right." I stopped on a sob. "God, I need You. . . . Jesus, You've got to help me." I let the tears flow down my cheeks unchecked, begging for mercy.

The words didn't change my circumstances—my emotions were still in turmoil—but the request had been made. I stood quietly with my eyes tightly shut. Slowly, the stream of tears abated, their tracks drying on my cheeks. My heart was heavy, but the small step of faith taken to ask Jesus for help encouraged me.

I breathed deep, and a quiver ran through me as I exhaled. I was emotionally exhausted. I blinked, feeling a remaining drop of wetness leave my lash and splash onto my cheek. Numbly, I raised my palm and gently wiped the dampness away. I sniffed. I shuddered and took another trembling breath as I turned toward the exit door.

I stopped. I knew I couldn't leave without seeing David one more time. "God, help me," I breathed.

As I opened the door and walked into David's room, I held my breath. None of the past few minutes seemed real. I was still suffering from shock; my feet and my legs moved of their own accord.

My eyes slowly moved around the room. The pillow that I had brought earlier was sitting in the chair, untouched. I turned to the lone occupant of the room, hoping and half expecting my fears would be allayed.

David moved sporadically, an arm and then a leg thrust out with no regard for order. A moan escaped his throat; it was low and guttural, almost animal-like. The sound shivered down my spine.

His head snapped around. An avalanche of gibberish spilled out of his mouth. His legs moved again, wild and frantic. His arms twitched painfully, pushing in a frenzied motion. Then David's eyes opened, piercing me with emptiness. His head swung away, his eyes bouncing off my face.

David was even worse than I had remembered. The mind that had once operated with computerlike accuracy was now short-circuiting, completely out of control. Nonsensical words continued to pour from David's mouth, on and on and on.

I walked to David's bed to tell him I was going home. I touched his shoulder, but there was no response. He continued talking erratically,

Chapter Three

saying nothing and writhing on the bed—shifting, struggling like a fly caught in a web, unable to break free. He didn't hear me, he didn't feel me. His fever-reddened lips stood out in stark contrast to the pasty white pallor of his skin. His uncut brown hair was darkened with sweat, sticking out in awkward peaks.

What is going on in David's body? What is he feeling? What is causing him to throw himself around the bed . . . pain? How much is he suffering? The questions seeped through my numbness. *What is going on in David's mind? Does he know what is happening to him? Are his struggles efforts to free himself from painful torture, or is his mind oblivious to the battle, completely dominated by some virus?*

I stood silently by David's bed. The questions remained unanswered. Then appalling thoughts cut through my wondering: *David is probably fighting for his life! Who is winning? . . . Is David strong enough to resist?*

I turned and bolted from the room.

The stagnant air of the hospital corridor did little to relieve my nearly smothered senses. I craved fresh, cool air. I needed to breathe. I moved toward the exit doors to get out of that sterile, stifling hospital.

On my way home, I stopped and picked up the girls at the Erickson's home. Trying not to alarm my daughters, I told my friends what had happened to David with buried emotions. They invited me to stay with them for a while and to have dinner with them. They were offering me their companionship. I refused. Just the thought of food nauseated me and I needed solitude. I needed to get home.

Once I got home, I walked into our bedroom. I sat down on the bed, relieved to be off my feet. The entire day took on a surreal quality, like a bad dream. I closed my eyes. I took a deep breath and opened my eyes again. My gaze immediately fell on our bed. The empty space where David's pillow usually rested grabbed my attention.

David was gone.

At once I pushed the chilling thought aside. I took a deep breath, reigning in my feelings. I rose from the bed and fled from my thoughts.

I clicked into automatic, going through the mechanics of everyday life. Dinner for the girls and putting them to bed was accomplished

Awakened

without much fanfare. I buried my doubts and fears behind a mask. My façade was of a mother in control, so my daughters went to bed in peace. But once the girls were in bed, the thoughts that I had held at bay could be held back no longer. I felt completely helpless and empty.

I was on my own: David was delirious, . . . my parents were out of state, . . . David's parents were consumed with their own anxiety, . . . and my daughters were too young to understand the devastation threatening our family. There was no one to whom I could turn. I felt totally isolated. We didn't even have a pastor. The pastor of the church where we attended had recently resigned, and his replacement had not arrived yet. Even Dr. Lehmann was going to David's parents as David's immediate caregiver, because they were the ones who had contacted him for help.

On all sides I felt like I was fighting suffocating loneliness. I even felt like God had abandoned me.

I stood up and started pacing the floor.

I was confused and vulnerable. I wrapped my arms around myself, vainly trying to warm my chilled heart.

Through a watery haze, my eyes landed on my Bible laying on my nightstand. A pinprick of my conscience touched my soul. I knew God was the answer to my loneliness. The words written in the Bible told me He was with me, I just had to believe it. But I didn't know how. How do you approach God when you have something this devastating in your life . . . when you only seem to have the head knowledge He is there? How do you change the head knowledge into genuine faith and trust in God? How do you generate confidence when you feel abandoned and betrayed?

You don't.

I leaned back against the wall. "Oh, God," I cried. Anguish engulfed me to the point of almost physical pain, and my eyes overflowed with hot, bitter tears. Slowly, I brought my hands up to my temples and my fingers overlapped my forehead.

"I can't do it," I sobbed. "I can't work up enough faith on my own to believe in Your control of my life. I can't even feel You—Where are You?"

I was experiencing feelings so strong, so overpowering, that I felt like I was drowning.

"God, why is this happening? What have I done? What has David done? How have we failed?" The questions shot at heaven like blazing bullets, slamming into their target with fear and frustration.

Chapter Three

My back began to slowly slide down the wall, inch by inch. I leaned forward and sank to my knees. Nothing in my brief span of years had prepared me for this moment.

The room was silent. I heard no voice. I had no answers.

Eventually, the torrent of thoughts slowed to a trickle and then died into silence. I sat on the floor, seemingly lifeless, hunched over, with my head in my hands. I felt empty and exhausted.

Extremely vulnerable, I was losing the battle for faith. I was tired and worn out. I raised the white flag and surrendered.

"God, I am unable to bear this. . . . I can't do it. If You are here, . . . if You are in control, then I need to know it. I can't do this on my own. I need Your help!"

My gaze returned to my Bible, and I reached for it. David had taught me that God's Word could be trusted.

I flipped through the pages, stopping at Hebrews 13:5. It read, "For He Himself has said, I will never leave you nor forsake you." I noticed that the words were a quote from the Old Testament, so I looked at the reference in the margin to see if I could find where those words had been said before. I turned to the verses in my Bible: "Be strong! Be courageous! Do not be afraid of them! For the Lord your God will be with you. He will neither fail you nor forsake you" (Duet. 31:6 TLB). "Don't be afraid, for the Lord will go before you and will be with you; he will not fail nor forsake you" (Duet. 31:8 TLB). ". . . I will not abandon you or fail to help you" (Josh. 1:5 TLB).

I went back to Hebrews and read on. "The Lord is my helper; I will not fear. What can man do to me?" The margin again gave other scriptures for me to read: Psalm 27:1 and Psalm 118:6.

> The Lord is my light and my salvation; whom shall I fear? When evil . . . come[s] to destroy me, [it] will stumble and fall! Yes, though a mighty army marches against me, my heart shall know no fear! I am confident that God will save me. . . . Listen to my pleading, Lord! Be merciful and send the help I need. (Ps. 27:1–7 TLB)

My eyes fell on chapter 31, and it was like I had written the words:

> Lord, . . . don't let my enemies defeat me. Rescue me because you are the God who always does what is right. Answer quickly when I cry to you; bend low and hear my whispered plea. Be for me a great Rock of

safety from my foes. Yes, you are my Rock and my fortress; honor your name by leading me out of this peril. . . .

O Lord, have mercy on me in my anguish. My eyes are red from weeping; my health is broken from sorrow. I am pining away with grief. . . . I stoop with sorrow and with shame. . . . Everywhere I looked I was afraid. But I was trusting you, O Lord. . . . Don't disgrace me, Lord, by not replying when I call to you for aid. . . .

Hide your loved ones in the shelter of your presence, safe beneath your hand. . . . Blessed is the Lord, for he has shown me that his never-failing love protects me like the walls of a fort!

I spoke too hastily when I said, "The Lord has deserted me," for you listened to my plea and answered me.

Oh, love the Lord . . . , for the Lord protects those who are loyal to him. . . . So cheer up! Take courage if you are depending on the Lord. (Psalm 31:1–24 TLB)

I turned the page to Psalm 118, reading; "In my distress I prayed to the Lord and he answered me and rescued me. He is for me! How can I be afraid? . . . The Lord is on my side, he will help me. . . . It is better to trust the Lord than to put confidence in men" (Ps. 118:5–8 TLB).

The meaning of the promises penetrated into my mind and deep into my soul. The Lord *was* with me! God's Word had spoken it.

No human reasoning could explain the change that took place in my heart. A miracle had transpired. God's Word sustained me and ministered life to me. A God-given assurance sprung from the depths of my spirit, and a confidence in God's continual presence poured over me. I was different. I no longer felt alone.

"Thank you, Jesus," I breathed.

Then the Lord spoke to my heart, gently but firmly expressing His love to me, affirming His faithfulness and assuring me that He was with me.

I basked in God's presence, amazed and in awe at His provision.

The questions posed in the lyrics of a song floated across my mind.

> Are you tired of chasing pretty rainbows?
> Are you tired of spinning 'round and 'round?
> Wrap up all the shattered dreams of your life,
> And at the feet of Jesus lay them down.
>
> He never said you'd only see sunshine,
> He never said there'd be no rain.

Chapter Three

> He only promised us a heart full of singing,
> At the very thing that once brought pain.
>
> Give them all, give them all, give them all to Jesus:
> Shattered dreams, wounded hearts, broken toys.
> Give them all, give them all, give them all to Jesus,
> And He will turn your sorrow into joy. [4]

Well, I didn't know how the promised joy would become a reality, but I did realize that it was my choice whether or not to give my shattered dreams and my wounded heart to Jesus. Then, the "joy" part I could leave to Him.

I stood up and reached my hands toward the heavens, choosing to give my burdens to Jesus. I felt my sorrow lift. He was doing what He promised: Jesus was shouldering my burden and lightening my load.

I closed my eyes and praised the Lord.

I was slowly beginning to really trust Jesus. I was believing in His guiding hand like I had never done before, and to trust Him when everything around me pointed to devastation and despair. I was only scratching the surface, but I was beginning to realize that I could place my life in His hands and completely rely on Him to be with me, as well as make all things work together for good.

I could sense Jesus' hand in mine, and I felt the first stirring of hope. The tears still flowed, but, this time, the tears combined with praise to my God, my Savior, my Healer—David's Healer. My praise ascended into heaven, and I went to bed that night with confidence that the hand of the Lord was upon David and me. I rested in God's power and sovereignty.

My head touched my pillow, and I instantly fell asleep.

The next morning, October 13, I woke up dazed. I blinked my eyes, trying to focus them. David's pillow was gone—and so was David. My memory of the previous day hit me like a blow. I reeled from the impact. I climbed out of bed, shaking off the last remnants of sleep. The peace and comfort of the night before seemed somewhat distant in the harsh light of a new day, and I begged for help.

Awakened

"God, I need You," I cried, summoning all the forces of heaven to my side.

I borrowed Eric and Helen's car and drove to the hospital to see David. He did not seem any better, but I was definitely calmer. The miracle of sleep sustained me, and the recalled promises from God's Word upheld me. I knew Jesus was with me; the loneliness was gone. I was still afraid of what was happening, my circumstances seemed to be careening out of control, but I had newfound confidence in God's ultimate control. And, in that assurance, I survived.

David underwent more tests to try to identify the virus that was creating havoc in his body. The doctors were baffled. They jabbed and poked, pricked and probed every spot on David's body. Mystified by his condition, they trudged through a rule-out process. Frustratingly, every analysis came up negative. On paper, he looked completely healthy, so the diagnosis continued to elude them.

Orderlies came to take David for a skull x-ray, because the doctors wanted to see if they could, once more, try to find some clue to David's medical condition. But first the orderlies needed to put David in a wheelchair to transport him to X-ray. His arms stiffened as the men tried to get him into the chair. Then he lashed out. He threw his arms and hands into the air; his legs kicked and his body squirmed, struggling against the orderlies as they subdued him.

I bent down to see if I could help.

"David . . . " I whispered.

David didn't respond to me, but his hysterical jabber intensified.

I cleared my throat.

"David, honey," I tried again a little louder, hoping my voice would grab his attention.

David continued thrashing, his arms were like propellers. I jumped back, narrowly escaping his erratic movement.

I leaned over again, wanting to comfort him with my words. "David, they're taking you to X-ray. It will be OK. . . . I love you."

David didn't respond. He didn't even look at me. He just continued incoherently protesting the injustice of his capture.

Chapter Three

The orderly, with David tied in the seat, pushed the chair out of the room and into the hospital corridor.

As soon as they started wheeling down the hall, David's attitude completely changed. His disjointed, unintelligible mumbling transformed; it cut off in mid-garble. Instantly, the fight drained out of his limbs, and the orderlies relaxed their vicelike grip. David mutated from a disturbed man to a small, immature child just experiencing his first roller-coaster ride. He threw his hands in the air, oblivious to the growing crowd of spectators, and waved them wildly.

With an excited shriek, David cried, "Wheeeee . . ." He was so excited. He was consumed with the thrill of moving down the hallway. He was captivated by the rolling wheels beneath him.

I was devastated.

A staring crowd quickly gathered. I felt embarrassed by the startled looks. The gawking faces quickly masked to sympathy when they realized I was looking at them.

I watched the spectacle wheeling down the corridor slowly disappear, my legs unable to follow. David's ecstatic shouts grew fainter until the commotion finally faded away as they turned a corner. But his voice lingered in my head; echoes of his infantile delight replayed over and over in my mind.

"Oh, God . . ." My voice stopped, but my heart screamed for courage.

I closed my eyes, effectively cutting off my view of the dwindling crowd. Then I took a deep breath and opened my eyes. The impromptu circus was over. I was by myself.

I decided I would go home. I couldn't do any more here; David would be gone for the rest of the afternoon. I kept my gaze fixed straight ahead and walked down the hall. I pushed the call button for an elevator to take me to the main floor.

Desperately, I cried out to God, "Lord, I'm sorry, but I really need You to show me we are not alone. My mind tells me You are with us, and Your Word promises You will never abandon us. . . ." I paused, searching for the right words to express the tug of war taking place in my spirit. "I guess I just need some human warmth, someone to be able to lean on a little bit through this. . . . Would that be OK?" I hesitantly petitioned.

In front of me, the elevator doors opened.

Riding the elevator was a man. Still immersed in my own thoughts, I looked into his face without recognizing him.

"Mrs. Anderson?" His words floated toward me.

The man standing in the elevator smiled at me, and for the first time I really looked at him. It was Pastor Johnson. He pastored the Philadelphia Church in Ballard, one of the churches David's parents attended. On special occasions we accompanied my in-laws to his church, so he recognized me. He was a large, slightly balding gentleman with a most pleasant, serene expression on his face. I didn't know him personally, but I knew of him, and I had heard him preach. As he saw the recognition in my eyes, his smile widened, and he spoke again.

"Are you all right?" He questioned as I joined him in the elevator.

His smile was contagious, and I responded with a weak imitation of his. "Pastor Johnson," I eluded his inquiry. "Were you visiting someone?"

The look in his eye told me he knew I had evaded his question, but he responded to mine anyway.

"Yes." The kindness and love of the Lord went with this man. As the elevator descended, I could sense the presence of the Lord with us, and I drew strength from it.

The pastor saw the pallor of my face and the strain around my mouth. He seemed to sense my inner pain. His Scandinavian accent deepened with compassion as he repeated his earlier question. "Are you all right?"

I found myself responding to this man of God. His smile, his kindness, and his love for God drew out my explanation. My lips lifted in a slight, sad smile as I answered. "No, not really. My husband, David," I confided, "is in this hospital."

His face expressed genuine sympathy as I continued. "He is quite sick, but the doctors don't know what's wrong with him."

The elevator doors opened and we both stepped out. The pastor took my hand and pulled me aside to continue our conversation. His touch was the answer to my prayer. The warmth of his hand was like Jesus reaching out and touching me and telling me I was not alone. Here was proof there was someone who cared about what happened to me and what was happening to David.

As I poured out our story to Pastor Johnson, his eyes reflected empathy and he displayed the love of the Lord Jesus Christ to me. He promised that he would go to see David and pray with him. Then, before parting, he prayed with me.

Chapter Three

As I walked out of the hospital, I felt lighter. Nothing had really changed—no miraculous healing or spectacular answers to the hard questions that were troubling my mind—but the simple touch of a caring person was what I had needed to assure me someone did indeed hear and care. God was answering my prayers, one step and one touch at a time!

I went home, and God continued to answer my prayer. I received phone call after phone call from people who expressed their concern for me, David, and the well-being of our family. Good friends who attended our church offered to watch the girls as much as I needed. My sister, Sylvia, also offered to baby-sit the girls if needed. This would enable me to spend more time with David.

The support of the people in the church we attended was strong, especially from the young people. Up until the day he got sick, David had been involved with the youth group. He had even started a choir of young people. The youth group took David into their hearts, and they called to tell me that they were calling an all-night prayer meeting. They would pray for David's healing; they wanted to see David back on his feet again.

I found a half-written letter started by David to Bernhard Johnson, the missionary in Brazil where David had gone the year before with a ministry team. I sat down and read the letter. David had described the church he was working on. He told a little bit about the young people at church, and he had started relaying some personal facts about our family. But he had abruptly stopped halfway down the page, too weak to continue.

As I held the incomplete letter, words and phrases asking for prayer spun around in my mind. I picked up a pen and began to write. I told Bernhard that David had become seriously ill, that he was in the hospital, and that the doctors were at a loss as to the cause of David's illness. I ended the short note with a request for prayer on David's behalf. I sealed the envelope, comforted by the prospect of even more prayer rising to God for David's healing.

That evening, David's second full day in Ballard Hospital, I left the girls with friends from church and traveled back to see David again. Up to this point, the chemistry studies done on David had ruled out infectious

Awakened

mono. The hospital had taken skull and chest x-rays, and they all read as normal. This meant the doctors were functioning without a working diagnosis. And even though the doctors had stopped all medication, David was still disoriented and in pain.

I made my way down the hospital corridor and toward the nurses' station. The nurse caught my eye and smiled as she recognized who I was.

"Oh, Mrs. Anderson," she haltingly exclaimed. "How are you this evening?"

I knew that the nurse was awkwardly trying to fill the silence, in some small way trying to sympathize with the trauma unfolding in my life, so I gave her a smile and waited for her to continue talking. After a brief hesitation she continued.

"David's condition is holding steady. There has been no change since you were here this morning."

The nurse's words could only mean one thing: *David is still delirious.*

I murmured a quiet thank you. My heart plummeted as I turned away from the nurse. Inside, I was shaking. I braced myself for what I knew would be facing me behind the closed door of David's room.

I put my hand on the doorknob and turned it slowly. I took a deep breath, hoping to bolster my flagging courage, and walked into the room.

I could see the outline of David in his bed. Immediately, I noticed his relative stillness. He was completely different from the thrashing maniac I had seen the last time I had visited. He actually seemed somewhat calm. My heart contracted. My fingers flexed. *Don't get your hopes up too high, Joan,* I admonished myself, trying to quench the flicker of optimism that flared in my heart. I closed the door behind me and walked farther into the room. Moving closer to David's bed, I felt my heart lighten.

The closer I got, the more my expectations grew. I stopped a short distance away from David and looked over his face. His features were at rest, completely still. His skin tone was pale, with a somewhat putty hue, and it glistened with sweat. His breathing was labored but steady. Occasionally, his muscles twitched, contracting of their own free will. But it was nothing compared to the nightmare that had previously confronted me.

The room was quiet, only the sound of David's breathing touched my ears.

Chapter Three

I took a hesitant step closer and continued studying David's features. His gaunt face was framed by a dark shadow of unshaven stubble. No one had dared come close to him with a sharp razor in his delirious state. A hint of dampness glistened on his straight locks, evidence of the ever-present fever. Periodically, a slight moan would escape his dry, chapped lips, but his relative quietness touched a deep, hidden seed of expectancy buried in my heart.

His eyes were peacefully closed.

I closed my own eyes. I could feel the moisture gather behind my lids, and I tried to hold it back. "Thank you, God," I whispered. Gratitude mingled with cautious hope. I opened my eyes and stepped up to the bed. I bent to kiss my husband's cheek.

David's eyes flew open. His gaze pierced through me, and I froze in midmotion. Suddenly apprehensive, I swallowed. David's eyes never left my face yet they stared right through me, dazed and confused. It was unnerving.

Irritation flashed in his eyes. His face bounded away from me. His eyes ricocheted around the room, scanning everything. He squirmed, showing remnants of his maniacal behavior. His gaze desperately touched everywhere, as if searching for something.

What was going on? There was something ominous in David's silent search.

Slowly, his nose started to twitch and a funny, almost crazy gleam flared in his eyes. He squinted, and his head began to rock back and forth. His body flinched away from me, his hands batting at the bed linen. A deep, guttural moan started in his chest. Finally, in disgust, he spat out an accusation.

"You stink!"

My jaw dropped. I was stunned. "What?" I breathed.

"Phew! Get away."

I jerked away from David's bed before my mind even had a chance to assimilate David's words. The line of his mouth was thin and hard. A painful fire blazed in his eyes. I shrank away from the agony on David's face.

"Oh, . . . I'm sorry," I stammered. I gulped tightly, completely appalled by the turn of events. My sense of shock was paralyzing. David's words repeated over and over in my head, *You stink. You stink. . . .*

Awakened

Ice dripped from his mouth. The utter disgust and repulsion in his voice was overwhelming and scathingly brutal. This did not sound like David. His sense of smell and social graces had to be distorted by the illness he was fighting. *How much of David would be attacked by this persistent monster?*

Again, David scrunched up his nose, this time waving his hands spasmodically in front of his face. He grunted, "You really stink." His tone was a little louder. His eyes looked feverish, and he was visibly shaking. His obvious distress jolted me into action.

Turning abruptly, I moved to the other side of the room. My eyes darted back and forth, trying to find something, anything that could be causing the stench. I spotted some flowers given by family and friends and grabbed the vases. Stacking these by the door, I moved them as far away from David's bed as I could. A fine sheen of perspiration broke out on my forehead.

David didn't stop. He batted and slapped at the invisible enemy, swinging his arms to fight the offensive odor.

I took a deep breath, inhaling through my nostrils. I smelled the air, trying to identify the source of David's hysteria. I couldn't isolate anything that could possibly cause David's severe reaction.

"Phew, phew, you stink. Get away! Get away. . . . Leave me alone." David coughed, almost gagging on the words.

I looked at David again. I was shocked to see that all the color had drained from his face. His eyes were dark with desperation. He moaned and thrust his head from one side to the other.

I sniffed again, longer and deeper, closing my eyes to concentrate as much as possible. I cupped my hand in front of my mouth and blew into my palm, sniffing—nothing. I tried to bend as close to my armpit as I could. Nothing, except maybe a hint of deodorant. The lingering fragrance gave me an idea. I lifted my wrist to my nose and sniffed. *Maybe . . .* I smelled my other arm. *Could it be my perfume?* David had always liked this particular fragrance, but the fevered man laying across the bed was not really the David I knew. Maybe my perfume was the cause of his distress.

I abruptly swept the room with my eyes one final time. It seemed there was no other possible cause for David's distress.

Chapter Three

Finally, unable to withstand David's hysterical command for me to leave, I obeyed. Grabbing the flowers in one huge armload, I walked through the door.

I have to tell someone, the insistent thought intruded with frantic persistence. *Now!*

My pulse refused to behave normally, racing when I desperately needed to remain calm. As I reached the nurses' station, the nurse on duty turned toward me with a smile. Her smile faded as she saw me. Standing before her was a frantic woman carrying an armful of flowers, complete with a pasty white complexion and frightened eyes. She opened her mouth to say the expected platitudes when I simultaneously found my voice.

"Are you all right?" she said, her concern evident.

"I need to see a doctor right away," I interrupted, ignoring her inquiry.

"Calm down, Mrs. Anderson," she soothed. My eyes communicated my distress. "I'll see what I can do."

I desperately longed to sit down. I felt a sudden loss of energy. So like an automaton, I maneuvered my way into the lounge to wait for the doctor.

"Mrs. Anderson?" the doctor whispered.

I turned toward the sound.

The doctor's eyes were filled with compassion and shared human warmth. He smiled. Sitting down next to me, he asked me why I needed to see him.

Haltingly, I began to explain what I had encountered in David's room. As I talked, the doctor's manner changed from compassion to concern. I finished by explaining how I had searched myself and the room for odors and removed the flowers.

"You did the right thing," he reassured.

I glanced at him gratefully, thankful for the comforting words.

Then, decisively, the doctor stood up.

"I'll have to examine David myself." The doctor's lips tilted upward as he continued. "I'm sure we will find an explanation for his problem—apart from yourself."

Appreciating his humor, I smiled a little sheepishly.

"Thank you," I whispered.

Awakened

He smiled and left the lounge.

―※―

The doctors at Ballard Hospital, including Dr. Lehmann, were still totally baffled by David's condition. Test after test proved futile in leading to a diagnosis. David stayed delirious. His fever remained high, and the mysterious odor continued. The only conclusion they offered was that whatever was plaguing David was leaving a "calling card"—a potent, nauseating odor that only David could smell. Nothing the physicians tried helped. There seemed to be no relief for the fever and, therefore, nothing could bring him out of his delirious state.

Finally, on October 14, his third day at Ballard Hospital, Dr. Lehmann decided to transfer David to the University of Washington Hospital. At the University, more in-depth research and investigation could be performed to discover the cause of David's virus.

Chapter Four

David was placed on a stretcher and wheeled to an ambulance. He was still disoriented, loud and "silly." He remained feverish.

I rode with David in the ambulance, and he mumbled the entire trip, rambling on and on—confused and irrational. I was totally ignored unless I got too close, then I was quickly reminded that my presence bothered his nose.

Once admitted to the University of Washington, Dr. Lehmann handed David's chart over to the staff. A letter described the course of treatment he had received at Ballard Hospital:

> Mr. Anderson was admitted to Ballard Hospital on 10-11-65 with the chief complaint of malaise, sore throat, generalized fever with chills, which had been present for three weeks prior to admission. He was placed on sulfa drugs through his medical carrier. He continued to exhibit temperature and fever and, about a week later, the attending physician during his stay at Ballard Hospital was called (James H. Lehmann, MD).
>
> At that time, he complained of dizziness, nausea, and vomiting. A diagnosis of labyrinthitis was made. He continued to show further febrile elevations and became more toxic and also weaker,

Awakened

until he was given Tigan and an injection of penicillin. His admission diagnosis to the hospital was acute mononucleosis.

Physical examination revealed mild injection of the throat. Other than that, the examination was completely unrewarding.

A copy of the laboratory findings is enclosed for your perusal. A culture of the cerebral spinal fluid revealed no growth in 48 hours. A gram stain revealed no bacteria.

X-ray films of the chest and skull have already been sent to you under separate cover. The reports of same were normal.

On his third hospital day, Mr. Anderson was transferred to your care.

Sincerely,
Medical Records Librarian
Ballard Hospital

The first item on the University of Washington doctor's agenda was to get David's medical history. They sat me down and pumped me for information. Their chart began:

This is the first admission for this 29-year-old white male, who was admitted 10-14-65 with a fever of 3–4 weeks duration. He is a civil engineer living in Seattle who was in excellent health until 3 weeks ago.

Religious, family man. No smoking or drinking. He was in Brazil 1+ year ago for 3 months; had several episodes of dysentery and parasitic worm infections (picked worms from beneath skin—larva migrans). He had had all his shots prior to leaving, but has had only 1 polio shot 6 years ago.

Two of 3 daughters had a 24-hour bout of fever, nausea, and vomiting; no sequelae.

On the day prior to admission, he suffered a bee sting.

Working in a swampy area prior to the onset of his illness and was bitten by numerous mosquitoes.

History of Present Illness:
- Admitted to Ballard Hospital where a test for mono was negative.
- He had skull films, malaria smear exam, CSF.
- He was given penicillin shot.

- He was treated with aspirin, ? antibiotics, and within 24 hours had severe vomiting, generalized stomach pain and headaches, and shaking chills. He was very agitated and was transferred to U.H.
- He has had 10-pound weight loss (175–165) in past 3 weeks.
- He has had no recent skin rash, and has had no bowel movement since last Monday.

Past Medical History:
- Patient had a duodenal ulcer 16+ years ago, which was treated medically. He had a peptic ulcer 7 years ago in Navy. He still occasionally has attacks of hyperacidity, but has had no other symptoms.
- Patient had an auto accident 13 years ago, knocked unconscious.
- No family history of genetic disease.
- Usual childhood diseases; however, does not know for certain whether he ever had mumps.
- He has had no previous similar illnesses or hospitalizations.
- No known allergies.
- No malaria.

Once the questions were answered to their satisfaction, the physicians began, once again, to try to identify the illness that was eating away at David. They did a thorough physical examination: They took his vital signs, checked his skin for rash, and felt his neck. They inspected his eyes, ears, and throat. They listened to his heart and lungs, felt his abdomen, and checked his neurological functions. In general they saw "a confused, disoriented, white male who answered questions inappropriately."

David had a few nodes in his neck. His heart sounded good, with no murmurs or friction. His abdomen was soft, but there was "minimal tenderness over the liver" and bowel sounds were hyperactive. David also had "mild thigh discomfort on bilateral leg extension, suggestive of a meningeal irritation." His thrashing and fitful discomfort, they concluded, was due to pain. At this time, the only logical source of this pain was the drugs he was on to try to reduce his fever. Consequently, the doctors stopped all medicine. Furthermore, David's cranial nerves were intact, as well as his sensory nerves. He had no muscular weakness or atrophy. And all reflexes were present.

In short, there wasn't much to go on.

Then came the laboratory tests: "hematocrit, sed rate, WBC, urinalysis, lumbar punctures, blood cultures, stool guaiac, heterophile test." And chemistries: "electrolytes, BUN, SGOT, SGPT." Then came the EEG, which resulted in "an abnormal pattern suggestive of a diffuse disturbance of brain function with a focal sign over left anterior and midtemporal regions."

The tests were possibly beginning to pay off, and a general working diagnosis was made: viral encephalitis—or, inflammation of the brain due to a virus.

One of the tests conducted on David was a spinal tap, or lumbar puncture. This is a laboratory serologic test, a study of antigen-antibody reactions, of the spinal fluid. A long needle is inserted into the vertebral column in the lower back and the spinal fluid is drawn out. This test is excruciatingly painful. As the needle penetrates the spine there is normally a physical reaction that includes the patient's muscles contracting as the body stiffens in response to the pain. Once inside, the needle causes temporary but complete paralysis in the patient; therefore, no painkiller is used. The lack of medication also ensures complete purity of the serum.

When David was given this test, his reaction was completely abnormal: The needle was inserted, and he lay motionless on the table. No muscles jumped, no sweat broke out on his body, and there was no nerve response. The medical personnel were shocked. His indifference to the pain was completely unexpected.

The results of the test were completely negative, the spinal fluid culture was clean of any virus. This same test was administered twice with the same result: No response to the pain and no proof of viral activity.

Other tests came back negative as well, and the doctors became even more confused. There was no objective evidence of the virus that was inflaming David's brain.

During these days, I existed minute to minute. Miraculously, every night I would fall asleep as soon as my head hit the pillow. But occasion-

Chapter Four

ally, in the middle of the night, I would wake up with my stomach growling. I was losing weight and had dropped about 15 pounds. I couldn't face the thought of eating. I would close my eyes and ignore the demands of my body. And then, in the morning, I would go back to the hospital to renew my vigil after a token amount of food.

David's restless, erratic behavior was diminishing, even though his fever still burned. Ever since the doctors stopped all medication, David actually had periods of quietness. But the slightest things unnerved him, and he became agitated easily. The one thing that would settle him down was if someone prayed with him. At these times, David almost became lucid. His speech cleared, and he praised God coherently.

David's father and mother were among those who came to the hospital to pray. With each visit, however, Helen became more frustrated at the lack of David's recovery. She felt out of control of the situation. She would try everything she could think of to get him to snap out of his delirium, but he wasn't cooperating. The tone of her voice would intensify with her efforts. David was seemingly oblivious to her, but the tension in the room was real, and the stress pressed through to him. David's body would grow taut, and he would thrash more than usual.

The doctors saw a correlation between David's agitated conduct and having visitors. Consequently, they posted a *No Visitors* sign on David's room. When they explained the notice to me, I had the distinct impression they had a certain visitor in mind. But since the posted restriction technically applied to nonfamily members, we could only hope it would serve to minimize Helen's visits.

By Sunday, October 17, after David had been in the University Hospital three days and had undergone many tests, the doctors had some limited information for me. Until now they had stayed uninformative with their comments. "We're still running tests," and, "We're doing the best we can for David," were running a close race as to which statement was the most used response to my questioning.

David had been seen by the Neurology and Infectious Disease departments, as well as the attending physicians. He had had brain scans

Awakened

and spinal taps and x-rays. Every secretion from his body had been tested and retested. But a firm diagnosis still eluded the doctors.

At this point, the only way to find out what was wrong was to rule out what wasn't. And the rule-out strategy was providing some insight. The doctors were able to say with some confidence that David did not have spinal meningitis—a virus accompanied by fever and acute pain that affects the nerves and inflames the meninges of the spinal cord. They ruled out mumps, bee-sting reaction, and peptic-ulcer disease. They also ruled out frightening possibilities, such as a brain abscess or tumor and poliomyelitis. The only time the doctors felt confident was when they spoke of what was *not* influencing David's condition. This was a small crumb of comfort, because they had not found the real cause of David's illness. The doctors still considered encephalitis as a possibility. For that, there was no cure.

The worst-case scenario was that David would remain as he was and eventually die. If by some miracle his fever did go down, David would likely be a human vegetable. He had been in a delirious state with a high fever for so long it was probable the high temperature had totally incinerated everything that made David who he was. The doctors gave me no hope. To them, the most optimistic prospect was that David would die and not have to live a life without a mind.

That afternoon, I went home alone and very, very weary. It was all I could do to drag myself up the single flight of stairs to the apartment we called home. *I'm so exhausted!* I thought as I paused to insert my key in the lock. *I guess I'm in shock.* Not for the first time, I wished I could lie down and sleep, waking up to discover that the past few weeks had been just a terrible nightmare. But I couldn't. I still had to check on the girls. I needed to call my parents and update them on David's condition and the lack of a cure, or of even a concrete diagnosis. I needed . . .

I needed to get my shoes off.

I felt too tired and too dispirited to think clearly. I slowly made my way through the house to the bedroom. The house felt unnaturally still. I paused outside the door and fumbled for the light switch. I desperately tried to block out all thought of the hospital, of David, of the doctors

Chapter Four

groping for answers that just weren't there. I moved across the room and stopped in front of my mirrored dresser. Looking up, I saw my own face. Blank eyes stared back at me, eyes void of emotion, expressionless.

My hand landed on the hairbrush sitting on my vanity. I dropped my gaze to the hair set, and I remembered David giving it to me, . . . David's loving smile, . . . David's hands in my hair, . . . David; . . . David thrashing alone on a hospital bed, . . . David a vegetable, . . . David dead?!

No! my heart screamed.

Suddenly, I felt afraid—so terrified that the short hairs on the back of my neck stood on end. My heart ricocheted against my ribs, and I realized I was being swallowed by fear. I dropped the hairbrush on top of the vanity and gripped the corner with my hands, fighting waves of panic. I felt as though I was being swept along by an uncontrollable current in a churning sea.

I clasped my arms about my stomach. It was hollow and slightly nauseated from the upheaval of my emotions. I sucked in a short gasp of air, and it left my lungs with a broken sob of emotional pain. I felt like I had something precious, something wonderful, but I couldn't keep it. My hopes, my dreams, my love were being ripped away from me.

I crumbled under the pressure.

Without knowing how, I found myself on my knees, shoulders stooped, head bowed as if in prayer.

"Jesus . . ."

The divine name escaped my lips in a cry for help. "Oh, God, please don't let David die!" My anguished petition rose to heaven. My heart was heavy. I couldn't imagine life without David. And I couldn't begin to comprehend what being a widow at twenty-seven with three young children would be like. I couldn't do it!

Suddenly, my thoughts crystallized and I realized what I was doing. I was still trying to cope on my own, unconsciously struggling to carry my own burdens. I was startled by the flash of sadness this thought brought. If only I would remember to lay my burdens at Jesus' feet and leave them there.

I felt like there were chinks in my spiritual armor leaving me vulnerable and alone. I was like a child trying to learn how to swim, grappling with swirling currents and crashing waves when all I had to do was let Jesus calm the water to a peacefully smooth swimming pool. Gently, Jesus spoke to my heart, "Joan, bring your burden to Me. Let Me carry it. . . ." Right on the tail of this impression came assurance: *I could have peace right now, in the midst of my storm.*

"Oh, Jesus," I cried. "I'm sorry. . . . Forgive me. . . . Take my burden." No other words were needed.

> What a friend we have in Jesus,
> All our sins and griefs to bear!
> What a privilege to carry
> Everything to God in prayer!
> O, what peace we often forfeit,
> O, what needless pain we bear,
> All because we do not carry
> Everything to God in prayer!
>
> Have we trials and temptations?
> Is there trouble anywhere?
> We should never be discouraged,
> Take it to the Lord in prayer.
> Can we find a friend so faithful
> Who will all our sorrows share?
> Jesus knows our every weakness,
> Take it to the Lord in prayer.
>
> Are we weak and heavy laden,
> Cumbered with a load of care?
> Precious Savior, still our refuge;
> Take it to the Lord in prayer.
>
> In His arms He'll take and shield thee;
> Thou wilt find a solace there. [5]

My situation did not change. My husband was still in the jaws of sickness, with death his best prospect, but doubt and despair were suddenly banished from my heart. A heaven-sent peace touched my emotions. Tears flowed from my eyes. Words poured from my heart to the heart of God.

"Jesus," I whispered, "help me . . ." I swallowed, relinquishing control.

Chapter Four

"Oh, God," I pleaded, "please heal David. Raise him up to testify of Your healing power. Touch him with Your nail-scarred hand. . . . Or . . . take him home. . . . Just, please, don't let him become a vegetable."

The magnitude of what I was asking God to do struck me, and I reeled from the impact. I was actually releasing David into God's care—even if it meant death. I breathed a sob in surrender.

"Jesus," I yielded, "I place David in Your hands. I can't even begin to understand all that is going on, but I trust You." I raised my hands in submission.

"David's life . . . my life . . . our future . . . I leave to You. I love You, Jesus."

I worshipped Him in a familiar song with words that were now real.

> In my brokenness,
> In my hour of darkness,
> I will lift my hands and worship You.
>
> In my brokenness,
> In my time of sadness,
> I will lift my voice in praise to You.
>
> Time stands still as I kneel down before You.
> Life draws near, like waves upon the shore.
> You touch me.
>
> In my brokenness,
> In these whispering shadows,
> I will lift the pieces of my heart to You.
>
> I will lift my voice in praise to You.
>
> Time stands still as I kneel down before You.
> Life is here. Your waves of power and glory.
> Touch me.
>
> In my brokenness,
> In my hour of darkness,
> I will lift my hands and worship You. [6]

Awakened

I was not alone. I was not afraid. I lay down and slept. God's promise in Proverbs 3:24 became my reality: "When you lie down, you will not be afraid; yes, you will lie down and your sleep will be sweet."

The Sunday night prayer service at our church rang with praise to Jesus. The congregation was standing while the prayer request for David's healing was mentioned. A single voice then prayed above the cries for mercy and healing. A friend and teacher was lying sick in the hospital and only God, the Healer, could set him free. To God the assembly directed their petition and then their praise. For God alone could help, and God alone was worthy of their praise.

The soft wind of the Holy Spirit moved through a Brazilian chapel, gently stirring the seeking people. Their united cry rose upward and broke into heaven. Portuguese mingled with heavenly tongues ascended higher and higher, every heart expressing the same desire.

"Lord, God, heal David Anderson. Raise up the young man who came here to share Jesus with us and minister in song. Send your Spirit of life to breathe on him."

Their petitions, their cries, touched the ears of Almighty God.

In the stillness of an early autumn Sunday morning, Eric knelt in prayer. Darkness hovered around the corners of the room. An anguished groan escaped him—a sound from deep within his spirit, beyond the realm of words. Tears streamed down his face and dropped on his clenched hands. His lips moved in silent petition, pleading for the life of his son. His fingers slowly untwisted, and he shakily reached toward the Bible lying before him. His hands rested on the black leather and, with agony, he voiced the depths of his heart.

"Oh, my God, heal my son," he whispered.

Chapter Four

He stopped speaking, hoping for an answer to the cry of his heart. There was none. His eyes opened and rested on the precious book before him. His hands respectfully moved over the worn leather.

"Lord, why are You so silent? Speak to me. . . . Show me Your will."

He closed his eyes again. His hands grasped the edges of the Holy Book, and he bowed his head. Suddenly, he saw his son. In his vision, David was lying alone on a hospital bed, sick and still. He was whiter than his sterile sheets, and his life was slipping away. The room was quiet, nothing moved. David's face was pale, his eyes closed and his expression vacant.

Eric's eyes moved away from the face of his seemingly lifeless son, searching for some sign of hope. He spotted a book lying on David's chest. His interest ignited, he looked closer.

The book was worn. The tooled leather was black, with distinctive identifying marks: Faded gold lettering and a tattered ribbon bookmark; small water stains; a few uneven pages had escaped the original binding. Frayed corners testified of countless hours of use.

Eric recognized the book—his own Bible! The treasures and promises contained within it were familiar to him, yet he yearned for just one special word to bolster his faith.

Curious, He continued to examine the scene.

The Bible lay closed on David's inert body. The room was silent.

Uncertain, Eric's eyes strained to see through the Bible's cover. Longing swept through his heart as he struggled to understand what God was showing him. He tried to reach toward the book, to open its pages, hoping for some sort of promise from which to draw strength, or assurance of life. But he couldn't reach it.

Why was the book shut? God's Word was filled with promises of healing and life. So why was God showing him an unreadable book?

"Jesus! Why is Your Word closed?" he questioned. "Please, won't You open Your Word? Please, oh, please, I beg You! Give me a promise, a verse, a word—anything. . . . Please speak to me." With his head bowed and tears streaming down his face, Eric pleaded.

Then in the darkness of the early morning, he heard the still, small, sweet voice of Almighty God: *"My son, you do not need a new promise from Me. You already have everything you require. My Word rests on your son. It is not closed to keep you out; but My Word belongs to you in its entirety. You do not have only one verse from Me, but every promise con-*

Awakened

tained in My Word is yours for the asking; it belongs to you and your son. Take My Word, open it, and claim every promise. They are yours because you are My child! They are David's because he is My child!"

The vision faded. Eric, still on his knees, slowly opened his eyes. His gaze fell on his Bible still clasped in his hands. Its cover was wet with tears. God's every promise belonged to him, and he held them in his hands. Spontaneously, verses touched his memory:

"He sent His Word and healed them. . . ." (Ps. 107:20); "He has sent me to heal . . ." (Luke 4:18); ". . . pray . . . that you may be healed . . ." (James 5:16); ". . . and by His stripes we are healed . . ." (Is. 53:5); ". . . He will heal us . . ." (Hosea 6:1).

Every one of those words belonged to him, and Eric claimed each promise for David. The tears slipped over his lashes again, but this time they were tears of faith. His hands rose in the air as praise and thanksgiving came from his lips. His burden was lifted because he knew what no medical doctor could ever predict: David would live.

Chapter Five

L ight!
Bright, white, shining light. The light rays reached out toward David as he lay dying. They pulled him forward, leading him to their genesis. He was brought nearer. The inviting warmth beckoned. *I'm coming*, his mind cried. He would soon reach it. He strained for the source of the energy surrounding him. David tried to embrace the light and escape his painful body. He longed to touch the essence of the light, to bask forever in the life-giving rays. He yearned to reach the end of the tunnel, but something held him back.

David's forward motion suddenly ended. He lay suspended. Rays from the light still surrounded him. The molecules of light danced everywhere. They bathed him. They held him. David lay in the light, eyes closed yet seeing the brilliance. He could feel the warmth of the healing rays. There was such peace.

David's eyes blinked open. Light shimmered everywhere yet, somehow, it was dimmer than when his eyes were closed. He quickly closed his eyes again.

Yes, it was still there! The light was not gone.

Awakened

A feeling of comfort and peace radiated through David and warmed him. He sighed. He breathed deep, trying to draw in the light. Slowly, he opened his eyes again.

He saw undefined images. Sounds were muted. Everything he saw and everything he heard with natural senses was just a shadow compared to the brilliant presence of the light. David was drifting in the light.

God was present. God was touching him. God was the Light.

David closed his eyes again. The Light was slightly dimmer, but he was not afraid. He simply knew the Light would never be separated from him. Even though he had not reached the source of the Light, the Light would never leave him. He never had to be without the Light. With this knowledge, he rested. David gave in to the stillness around him. He slept—cool, comfortable, healthy sleep.

Chapter Six

I stepped off the elevator and surveyed the hospital corridor. It was Monday morning, October 18. I wondered if this day would be any different than yesterday, or the day before, or the day before that. In my heart, I knew *I* was different. A change had taken place in my heart last night when I prayed. *Jesus* was in control.

I was no longer drowning in despair and utter hopelessness. I could actually feel the prayers of our friends and loved ones. I knew my own prayers were being answered. The tears shed by so many on David's behalf buoyed me. I was reminded of the science experiment done by thousands of school-age children where an egg sinks to the bottom of a glass of freshwater yet floats in a glass full of saltwater. I felt like the egg. My storm-tossed sea had been miraculously transformed into an ocean full of prayer support. The tears of the saints lifted me. Amazingly, I was riding the waves of my stormy ocean instead of being submerged beneath the crashing surf.

I glanced at my watch: 9:30 A.M. The pseudo-normalcy of the morning flashed through my mind. I had already dressed and fed the girls and brought them to my friend Evelyn Erickson's home; they were set for their day.

Awakened

A small smile touched my lips as I thought of Doreen and Donna bouncing excitedly out of the car. They loved being at the Erickson's home; it was a treat. Their innocence touched my heart. It was a miracle how shielded they were, seemingly untouched by the tragic shambles of our circumstances.

My smile disappeared as a picture of Susan holding onto my leg flashed through my mind. A classic mommy's girl, she wasn't used to being separated from me. She was even more afraid, knowing her sisters would soon be taken to school. Her tear-streaked face pleading for me to take her along was fresh in my mind. I was torn by Susan's agony, yet I knew my place for today was to be in the hospital with David.

As I drew near the door to David's room, I noticed the door was shut. I glanced toward the nurses' station just as the duty nurse raised her head. Our eyes met and I smiled. Instead of the expected nod of recognition and reciprocated smile of the past few days, she hurriedly dropped what she was doing and shot out of her chair to intercept me. Seeing her hurried movements, I slowed my pace. I took a deep breath and braced myself for whatever was coming. *Can this nightmare get any worse?* my mind questioned.

"Mrs. Anderson . . ." she sputtered as she rushed to me.

Please, . . . no more, I mutely pleaded. But I clamped my lips together as a cool, controlled mask slipped over my features. I held the reins of my emotions with a tight hand.

The nurse visibly pulled herself together and professionally continued.

"Your husband's doctors have requested that you wait for them before entering his room." She swallowed and took a hurried breath before continuing. "There has been a change in David's condition, and the doctors are in with him now."

Speechless, I stared at her. The word *change* echoed in my mind. *A change? What does that mean? Oh, God,* my heart cried, *help me!*

I was vaguely aware of the nurse as she slipped back to her station. My mind whirled at the implication of her message. David changed. . . . Better? . . . Worse? *Oh, my Lord, how can it get worse? Is he dying?* The thought jolted through me like an electric current. The breath left my lungs in a surge of panic. Instantly, I was bombarded with dark, sinister images of a freshly prepared grave, lilies sprawled over a coffin, my chil-

Chapter Six

dren clinging to me and crying, the somber notes of an organ offering electronic comfort, myself dressed in black and alone—.

No! my mind screamed. I violently rejected the nightmare. *No, David can't be dying. He isn't dead!*

Sour bile rose in my throat, threatening to spill out. I was forced to swallow, and the acid churned inside me. I swung my head around looking for relief from the torment in my mind. My eyes focused on the door of the waiting area. The possibility of finding solitude there pushed me in that direction.

I stopped for a quick drink of water from the fountain near the room entrance. The cool stream dampened my tongue and brought relief to my nausea. I hung my head over the basin, my arms leaning on the cool, smooth chrome. I breathed. Slowly, I lifted my head and took the remaining steps to the waiting area. I sighed with relief when I saw the room vacant. I sat down and, closing my eyes, buried my head in my hands.

I breathed deep. The oxygen continued to relieve the nausea and clear my head.

Soon the hysteria of the moment began to fade as words of truth filtered through my panic. Words from my prayer time the night before splashed in front of my mind's eye—words of comfort, words of courage, words of hope. I recalled the gentle whisper of Jesus saying, *Joan, bring your burden to Me, let Me carry it. . . .*

The words covered my heart and mind with a familiar peace.

"Jesus . . ." I breathed.

Only one word, but it was the life-giving name of my majestic Savior. His name on my lips in my moment of need shattered my fear. *I can trust my God.* Assurance rose in my heart. *He is in control.*

Suddenly, the word spoken by the nurse seemed different. *Change.* The word had evolved into a glimmer of hope, from death to life, from darkness to light.

The room was crowded. All eyes were on the prostrate figure displayed on the sterile bed. David was completely still, motionless under their microscopic gaze. A sweat broke out on his brow. He could feel the wetness gathering around his temple, and he concentrated on the path

Awakened

of a bead of moisture as it trickled toward the pillow that supported his head. He looked around the room. A collection of nameless faces with piercing, hawklike eyes stared back at him.

David swallowed. *Where am I? . . . What is happening? . . . Who am I? . . .* He searched his mind. Tendrils of thought curled through his head, grasping for any shred of memory to connect him to the occasion in this room. Nothing! He closed his eyes in concentration.

Empty, . . . clean, . . . calm, . . . nothingness, . . . light—.

Light! He remembered the light, the peace. He began to breathe easier. The moisture ceased gathering on his temples as he began to relax.

"David!" The single word exploded in the stillness, shattering the calm, and David's eyelids jerked open.

His gaze forcefully connected with the eyes of the speaker. The bedsheets encircled him like a cocoon. He remained motionless.

"Do you remember me?" the nameless voice continued.

The question bounced around in his head. *Remember him?*

A flash of confusion burst across his face, but otherwise, he remained visually unaffected by the interrogation.

"Do you know today's date?" The voice paused, waiting for a response. "Do you know what year it is?"

David's fingers tightened into a fist, the only visible sign of his inner turmoil.

"Do you know who the president is?"

He sucked in his breath. The questions bombarding him were confusing and frightening. His eyes flitted back and forth, trying to focus on someone or something that could help him.

The examiner shifted from one foot to the other while he waited. Then his eye's lowered to the hard board he was holding.

David released the breath he had been holding.

"Do you know where you are?" the survey continued.

David blinked. He swallowed.

Finally, the doctor stopped quizzing David and gave information.

"You are at the University of Washington Hospital in Seattle, and I am one of your physicians. These doctors . . ." he gestured to the men surrounding the bed, "are also here to help you."

The words did nothing to relieve the confusion and hysteria building inside David. They were meaningless.

Chapter Six

The voice paused again as a quiet discussion emerged between some of the white-coated figures in the room. Heads bent together to confer. The heads nodded in agreement, then they broke apart.

One doctor came closer, breaking away from the others. He slowly raised one hand.

From his prone position, David lay watching the activity around him. A seed of curiosity began to grow, uprooting his apprehension. He watched the doctor float closer to him and he saw the hand rise, its fingers configured into a V.

"How many fingers am I holding up?" he asked.

"Two." David instantly responded. Immediately, shock jolted across his face, transforming his features. *How did I know that?*

"Good," the voice approved.

The doctor moved closer.

"David," the voice continued gently, "you have been very ill, and you may be feeling a bit disoriented. Don't worry, David. Its understandable and expected, and we are here to help you." He paused before finishing. "Do you have anything you want to ask me?"

Baffled, David shook his head, his mind not fully comprehending what the doctor had said.

The doctor, reading David's response as a negative, stood to his full height. Briskly, he concluded. "All right, David." He cleared his throat. "I know you are somewhat confused at the moment, but I would like to bring in your wife. Do you think you are up to that?"

David stared vacantly at the doctor. W*ife*? Bewildered, he lay on the bed. What . . . *wife?* David's instinct and reason had started to come to life.

This word is different! Why? David continued trying to analyze his awakened feelings. *I knew the answer to the last question about the fingers was two. How? That answer seemed to come from my head. . . . It was just there. But this word, wife, . . . I feel something different, something deeper.*

This feeling in my . . . my . . . I don't know, but . . . but I think I'm supposed to feel something. What is it? . . . How do I? . . . How do I . . . wife?

Beads of sweat glistened on David's forehead and dampened his hair. His bushy eyebrows drew together in a frown, and his eyes blinked. Wave after wave of helplessness washed over him. He was drowning in a turbulent sea of agitation. He turned his thoughts inward. He strained for knowledge but only felt discomforting emotion. The anxiety etched on his face went unseen as the doctor moved toward the exit.

Awakened

Help.

The desperate plea never left David's lips, yet the inner cry was heard in heavenly places. Mercy descended with the impression of words, *"I am here."*

He breathed deep, intuitively knowing the comforting words and the Light were one. A supernatural calm descended, pushing away the turmoil. His eyes closed in tranquillity.

How long I waited, I don't know, but eventually the door to David's room opened. I expectantly watched, waiting for the usual line of doctors and interns to file out of the room, their clipboards clasped in their hands and their white coats flapping behind them. Instead, one lone doctor stepped from the room and made his way toward me. I started to stand, but he motioned me back to my seat and then took the chair next to mine. I swallowed nervously.

"Mrs. Anderson . . ." he started, "there have been some new developments in David's condition."

I studied the doctor's face as he said those words. His features were professionally masked, all emotion hidden beneath the cool exterior. His hands were steady and he sat erect. He gave nothing away. My gaze focused on his eyes, trying to read beyond the professional façade. He sensed my scrutiny and smiled with friendly compassion.

"During the night, David's temperature stabilized, and . . . he came out of his delirium." He paused. A hint of confusion touched his features as he hesitated.

My heart jumped and started racing. *Did he say "out of delirium"?* "David is awake?" I stammered, voicing disbelief.

A smile touched the doctor's mouth. "Yes," he replied.

His eyes met mine in a shared moment of joy. I couldn't believe my ears.

"How?" I blurted.

The smile on the doctor's face fell, and the confusion I had only glimpsed earlier resurfaced. He cleared his throat and tried to professionally elude my question.

Chapter Six

"I am ordering some more tests, including another brain scan, to see if we can find the answer to your question."

His voice softened as he continued. "Right now . . ." he hesitated, "I would have to say David has experienced a remarkable turnaround; an unexpected development, to say the least." He paused again, searching for the right word. "Somewhat of a . . . a miracle."

A faint tint stained the doctor's cheeks, and he momentarily looked away, seemingly embarrassed at what he had said.

A miracle! The word danced from my head to my heart. *Thank you, Jesus,* echoed through my mind.

The doctor cleared his throat and continued.

"Well, as I said, David has come out of his delirium, but there is a slight problem." A frown creased his brow. "David is a little mixed up, and we need your help." He paused, making sure he had my full attention.

"You see, we need you to find out what he remembers and what he doesn't," he cleared his throat again, "sort of a little private detective work." He smiled self-consciously at his little joke.

I stared at him blankly, not sure what he meant. *Find out what David remembers?* I didn't understand.

The doctor continued. "David is awake and he knows you're here. He is expecting you to visit, in fact, he is waiting for you now. We didn't tell him anything about your children or family, because we want you to question him. Try to see what he knows."

The doctor stood. His hand motioned toward the door to David's room, gesturing for me to follow.

Puppetlike, I stood.

I don't remember walking, but I must have moved, because suddenly I found myself standing in front of the closed door. I knew David was inside, but I was apprehensive and unprepared to face him. The doctor's words had both excited me and made me uneasy. I didn't know what to expect. I breathed a deep, calming breath. I wanted more details about David's changed condition, but that apparently wasn't going to happen. I would just have to wait. It seemed the doctors themselves didn't know that much, anyway. For now, I would just have to be as much help as possible. David needed me to be strong.

The door was opened, and I was ushered inside.

I stood just inside the door of David's room and heard the latch click behind me. Tensely, I shrunk back at the sound, instinctively trying to

Awakened

escape. The muscles in my hands tightened, balling into a defensive fist. I could feel moisture in the center of my palm and the slight sting from my nails bruising my soft flesh. My nerves felt stretched. Initially, my gaze rested on the still figure in the bed. He was so quiet. My tension eased slightly.

Then, slowly, I became aware of the other people in the room. White coats were everywhere, and every eye was trained on me. I felt my face redden as I stood under their scrutiny. My legs trembled and my hands clenched again. My stomach flopped. *What am I supposed to do?* my mind agonized. I wanted to run, but my feet felt cemented in place.

Unexpectedly, I felt the hand of the doctor touch my back, gently urging me toward the bed where another doctor was whispering something to David. Miraculously, my feet obeyed his command and carried me forward.

David . . .

My eyes returned to my husband lying on the bed. He was staring at me, his eyes studying my face, absorbing every detail.

He was awake! My heart skipped a beat at the miraculous transformation. A smile hovered around my lips, the minuscule movement tilted the corner of my mouth, silently communicating my pleasure at the sight of my husband. I looked closer, studying him. David's face was no longer flushed—proof that his fever was gone. Yet, he looked so fragile. Nothing moved—no hand raised, no smile given. He just lay there, staring. It was eerie and strange with him so still and silent.

The room was quiet. Expectancy filled the air. The silence was oppressive. David lay like a mannequin propped up for display to the room full of examiners.

My apprehension escalated. My skin tingled from the touch of every eye in the room. No one moved. Every ear strained for my words. My mouth opened to speak, but nothing came out. I cleared my throat and tried again.

"Hello, honey," I summoned, my voice husky.

The syllables flowed across my tongue more easily than I had expected. I quickly glanced at the assembled crowd. Their eyes were now riveted on David, ready to analyze his response to my greeting. With the attention off of me for the moment, I began to relax. I turned my gaze back to David. *This is David,* I thought, *and he is actually looking at me! He is going to be all right.* My eyes misted over as I realized that what I

Chapter Six

and others had been praying for had happened. Right here in this room, God was working miracles. The magnitude of that thought left me breathless. I wanted to shout and clap my hands, but the scientific atmosphere kept my response in check.

David's lips opened to allow one word to slip out. "Hello," he responded.

The men surrounding the bed shuffled their feet slightly.

Knowing the doctors were expecting more conversation, I continued. "How are you feeling?" I paused, waiting for some kind of reaction. David didn't even blink.

The seconds dragged.

Finally, David responded.

"Fine." The single syllable left David's mouth in a low, gravelly breath.

I closed my eyes for a brief moment, basking in the wonderful, powerful feeling of being able to once again communicate with David. The incoherent gibberish was gone. The wonderful, awesome miracle was almost unbelievable.

The doctor's shuffled their feet again. The intrusive sound snapped my attention back to the task at hand.

Say something! I told myself. My mouth dried up. I tried to swallow. I didn't know what to say, and the presence of a room full of strangers enlarged the awkwardness.

"You look much better," I blurted, needing to fill the silent void. The words escaped my throat with a raspy sound.

Silence, . . . empty, hollow silence.

I held my breath. The clock ticked. Time evaporated. Every subtle nuance was observed by the doctors—every hint of movement, every gesture.

I broke out in a nervous sweat. My palms grew damp, and I could feel my slip sticking to my back. I swallowed. My eyes took in the entire room. Everyone was waiting, anticipating my next word. Then a slight movement of David's cheek muscle caught my eye. David was clenching his teeth. He was as nervous as I was!

I recalled what the doctor had said to me before stepping into David's room. These men were anxiously expecting me to get some sort of response from David. I was to try to get this lethargic, exhausted, uncommunicative person to interact with me. The doctors wanted anything. Any word, any emotion, any movement would be documented and later recalled for assessment and speculation. They were the technicians, and David and I were the lab specimens. No wonder David looked so pressured. My stomach was queasy. I swallowed. *Lord, help me.*

I breathed deep, letting God's peace flow over me. I flexed my fingers and wiped my palms on my skirt. Sighing, I knew I needed to resign myself to the scrutiny and inspection by the other occupants of the room. I knew they were there to help David, but I also knew I needed to block them out of my mind and concentrate on doing what they needed me to do: get David to tell me what he knows and what he remembers.

I closed my eyes and drew strength from within. I knew I was not alone; Jesus was inside me, guiding me and orchestrating my words. I opened my eyes again, this time consciously ignoring the surrounding physicians. I took another step closer to the bed and smiled at David. His eyes, once emotionless, brightened at my nearness. *Progress,* I thought. My heart lifted at this small success.

"May I sit down?" I asked, my hand gesturing toward David's bedside, my eyes never leaving his face.

"Yes." Another single syllable escaped David's reserve. His gaze swept across the doctors standing behind me. He seemed uncomfortable with their scrutiny, and he visibly swallowed. He had the doctors in full view, surrounding him, analyzing his every move.

Of course he is afraid, my mind answered. *Who wouldn't be?* Love welled up from inside me and reached toward David. I loved this man—this quiet, afraid man. I sensed his confusion and anguish, and I wanted to—I *needed* to—help him. The ten-year-old vow I made to David was never more real than at this moment. *I will be beside you in sickness....* I was here.

I reached out my hand toward David, needing to touch him, needing to communicate to him with more than just words. I needed his warmth, too. Our fingers touched, David stiffened, probably with embarrassment, but he didn't pull away.

His hand was cool and dry. Something was missing. His vitality, warmth, and strength seemed to be gone. Yet even though David was in an extremely weakened condition, his frail touch helped me to relax a little. I thought of more conversation.

"David," I started, "our girls wanted to come see you. They can't wait until you come home. Right now they are staying with our friends from church, Ray and Evelyn Erickson."

Chapter Six

I saw no sign of recognition from David.

"The Ericksons have been so kind and helpful while you have been here in the hospital. I don't know what I'd have done without their help." I summoned the courage to ask the question, "Do you remember the Ericksons?"

David's eyes bore into mine as he searched for the answer to my query. Then his lips parted. "No," he simply stated.

I swallowed and continued.

"Well, they are wonderful friends of ours. Our girls love to go to their home." My hand fluttered on my knee, clutching my skirt.

I drew in another breath and held it, searching for courage before asking the dreaded, unbelievably horrifying question. "Can you tell me the names of our daughters?"

I sucked in my breath as I waited for David's answer.

"No."

My breath escaped my lips, leaving my lungs as empty as my hope. *Oh, God, no!* The silent, anguished cry never left my lips. I tried to crush the rising panic and sense of despair that threatened to overtake me. I needed to find out if David meant he didn't remember our girls or if he just couldn't remember their names.

"Well, first there is Doreen." David stared at me with not even a hint of recognition at the name. "She is the oldest at eight. She is in third grade and loves school." A hint of Doreen's childlike impatience crept into my voice as I quoted her saying she couldn't wait for her daddy to come home. I smiled at the memory of her words.

David remained quiet and unresponsive.

"Do you remember Doreen?" I had to ask the question directly. I needed to know the implication of David's silence.

"No." The single word sliced through me.

Valiantly, I continued with our conversation

"Then there is Donna. She is our middle child, and she is five. She is in kindergarten and is already in love with school."

David's head slowly moved back and forth on the pillow. The slight movement communicated more than the one syllable word he had been using. His eyes began to droop slightly. His fatigue was becoming more and more evident. I continued quickly, needing to finish.

"Susan is our third child. She is the youngest at two. She is home with me all day and doesn't like to let me out of her sight. She's a real mommy's girl."

"No." The word emerged from David's lips before I even uttered the question.

His eyes drooped again, his heavy lids refusing to stay open much longer.

"Your parents will be visiting a little later today; I'm not sure what time."

His eyes touched mine. I could tell he heard me, but his fatigue was growing. I continued, "I love you. . . . The girls love you. . . . We miss you."

I quickly added, "Many people have been praying for you. Bernhard Johnson . . . do you remember Bernhard?" I paused for a brief second, hoping for a glimmer of recognition from David. His eyes stared blankly, not even a flutter of an eyelash.

In the tense, quiet atmosphere I heard the sound of pencils etching on paper as the doctors took notes. I could feel the pulse in my neck drumming out an anxious rhythm. My heart felt heavy, but I trudged on. "Well, Bernhard and his church members in Brazil have been praying for you. He called to say they have been holding all-night prayer meetings."

The memory prompted me to share with David the long list of praying friends and family.

"Others have been praying too. People from our church—the Tapperos, the Swansons, the Ericksons—the entire team from your trip to Brazil."

As I listed the names of our close friends, I continually expected to see a flash of response on David's face. Just a small spark of recognition would have been welcome, any movement at all. But nothing came. He stared at me and listened to me list off our closest friends and family members as if I were reading a list of names out of some phone book. My smile slipped, but I refused to lose heart completely.

"Your dad has been praying as well. He said he had a dream or a vision that gave him the assurance you would be well. Now, here you are, awake . . . and . . . Jesus healed you. . . ."

At the mention of the name of Jesus, David's hand squeezed my hand tightly and distinctly. His eyes and face remained unchanged, his only movement came through his hand. A response! David *knew* the name of Jesus.

I sat motionless as my heart lifted.

Chapter Six

The doctor, not seeing David's last response, placed his hand on my shoulder. I glanced his way, startled by his touch. His other hand motioned toward the door, signaling that it was time for me to leave.

"David," he spoke, "Joan will be back to see you again later. Now, I think you should rest."

I stood up, keeping my hand on David's. I didn't want to end this overdue contact. I didn't want to leave. "I'll be back soon," I reassured.

I looked at David and saw his eyes slide shut. It was then I saw the complete exhaustion etched on his features. Lines dipped into his face, a road map of sickness and frailty. David's breathing was shallow, his breath coming in short gasps that slowly grew deeper as he relaxed. I gently laid his hand down, my fingers lightly caressing his hand.

He was already asleep. Our conversation had completely drained him.

Quietly, I leaned over David. I placed a whisper of a kiss on his forehead, now cool and dry. The monstrous fever was gone. *Praise the Lord!* David's sleep was calm and he was still.

I moved away from the bed, thanking the Lord for helping David. Then I walked out of the room with the doctor behind me.

Without a word, the doctor joined the gathering group of white coats down the corridor and left me standing in front of David's closed door. They all seemed so absorbed in the mystery of David's illness.

Feeling abandoned, I tried to reassure myself. I remembered David's fingers tightening on mine at the mention of the name of Jesus. I knew that Jesus was David's only help.

Then, suddenly, images of David's eyes staring blankly at me at the mention of our girls flashed in my mind. People who David knew and loved seemed to have no emotional effect on him whatever. What was I to do? How could I help David?

Unexpectedly, the picture frame hanging on our bedroom wall came into my mind's eye. It had three pictures in a single frame, one of each of our daughters. David had made the frame to show off his "pride and joy." At that moment I knew what to do—pictures! I would go home and turn every page of every photo album we owned. I would search every photograph for evidence of David's past. Maybe, just maybe, the faces full of love and laughter would help restore David's mind.

That afternoon, I got out our most recent photo album and began flipping the pages. Some pictures were dismissed out of hand while others I struggled with, not sure if they held some significance for

David. As I studied yet another photograph, I felt the touch of a small hand, which drew me out of my thoughts. I looked up to see my daughter Doreen standing by my side, her hand on my shoulder.

"Mommy," her small voice inquired, "what are you doing?"

I looked into her innocent eyes and saw her simple curiosity. I smiled and answered the best I could without lying and without marring her innocence.

"I'm looking for some pictures to bring to Daddy. He wants to see pictures of you and your sisters, and his other friends and family."

"Oh." Her trusting eyes left mine to rest on the open photo album, her curiosity satisfied.

"Take this one, Mommy." Doreen's finger rested on a photo of me with all three girls wearing matching dresses.

"Why that one?" I asked, curious as to her choice.

Doreen smiled at me and sheepishly answered. "Because you look pretty."

As her last word died away, she turned and hopped out of the room. I watched her leave, touched by her words. I glanced down at the photo she had chosen and smiled. I picked it up and added it to my bring-to-hospital pile. It wouldn't hurt to look pretty for David.

Stairstepped and dressed alike, David's family—June 1965

When I stepped into David's room that night, I clutched my purse. The photos of our loved ones were bundled inside. I was nervous and hesitant, unsure of his reception of the pictures. Saliva filled my mouth and I swallowed. My lips felt slightly bruised from my worrying teeth. I inhaled a trembling breath and held it for moral support.

David was sitting up in the hospital bed, awake and alert. I looked into his eyes. In them I saw a hint of trust and expectancy. I exhaled on a sigh.

Slowly, I walked on trembling legs toward the bed. I wished I could sit down, I felt like my knees were going to give out. Surprisingly, with-

Chapter Six

out my voicing a request, David moved his legs slightly to one side of the bed, making room for me to sit. I hesitated, grateful for his thoughtfulness. Then I sat down. I swallowed again and summoned all the courage I could find in order to speak.

"Hi," I said. I couldn't believe that breathless voice was my own. I was nervous and afraid, afraid that my self-appointed mission would fail. I cleared my throat and tried again. I couldn't handle small chit-chat with my own husband, so I dove right into my mission.

"I brought some pictures of our girls for you to see."

No response.

The quiet was slightly awkward.

I clutched my purse, fumbling with the latch in an attempt to get the photos. David watched my bungling attempts without comment. I glanced at his face. He was emotionless, not even curiosity touched his features. It was as if he didn't know what I was doing. Finally, after what seemed like an eternity, my purse popped open and the bundle of photos lay within my reach. My hands touched the pile and I slid aside the rubber band holding them together. A photo of our three girls lay on top.

Our three girls, two months before David's illness—August 1965

A nostalgic smile touched my features as I separated this photo from the rest. I offered the photo to David. I wanted him to take it from me, but, at the very least, I wanted him to see it up close. My movement brought a completely different reaction from David than I expected. His face blanched, his mouth looked pinched, and dark fear dropped into his eyes.

I was stunned. Words froze on my tongue.

David's accelerated breathing could be heard in the suddenly quiet room. The frantic sound struck a compassionate cord in my heart. Sensing his fear, I moved my hand back a little, giving him space. At my withdrawal, David visibly relaxed, and I watched his eyes drop to the photo in my hand.

"These are our daughters," I pointed to each girl in turn, saying each name.

Awakened

He glanced once at the image in my hand and then his eyes jumped away. His face turned as white as the sheet surrounding him. His breathing accelerated again, his head turning slightly away from me. A slight sheen of perspiration appeared on his brow, evidence of his silent distress.

I set aside the photo of our girls with my heart sore. Silently, I reached for another. I refused to retreat completely. I may have lost the first battle, but the war was not over. The photo chosen by Doreen was next. It was the picture of me and our three girls all in a row. I picked it up.

David's eyes remained downcast.

I didn't speak for a moment, then I whispered, "Honey?"

His eyes met mine again after my softly spoken endearment. I held up the photograph, and this time David's eyes didn't turn away. He blinked, the only movement in the room.

"That's you," he stated matter-of-factly. His eyes were glued to the glossy surface of the snapshot.

"Yes," I encouraged. I was exhilarated.

One after another I passed the photos in front of David's face. I waited until I was sure his eyes focused on each one before moving on, but no other response was made. With a sense of uneasiness he continued to look but he did not respond. And as each picture passed in front of his eyes, my excitement diminished.

Family portrait taken before David's illness–1965

Achingly, the two of us stepped through our world snapshot by snapshot, each one familiar to me and foreign to David. His stressful gaze touched each image without even a flicker of recognition. As each frozen piece of history passed before him, my heart sank to new, uncharted depths. The David who knew and loved these people was gone.

Chapter Seven

On October 18—David's first day of his second life—everything was completely foreign to him. Even such simple tasks as eating were a challenge. On this day, the nurse came in with an order form for meals.

"This is the menu," she instructed. "Please make a mark next to the food of your choice." Business-like, she spat out the sentence as if the instructions were obvious. But to David, her statement triggered nothing but questions.

Vacantly, he stared at her, unable to put into words the dilemma created by the nurse's orders. Since he gave voice to none of the questions floating nebulously in his head, the nurse turned and left David alone with the menu and a pencil. He studied the paper and pencil in his hands. He searched his mind, waiting for some stored knowledge to help him.

Nothing!

He picked up the long, thin writing tool. Curiously, he examined the object. But there was still no spark of familiarity to aid his understanding. He breathed a soft prayer for assistance.

Then some unknown, buried reflex turned his hand toward the paper and caused him to press the pencil onto the surface. As his hand moved, a gray line emerged. Yes! This felt right.

Awakened

His eyes dropped again to the paper. He picked it up to handle and touch the smooth surface. His eyes encountered printed markings. They were stacked evenly; rows of black ink ran up and across. He sensed those letters were supposed to tell him something, but he wasn't sure how or why. He studied the markings, trying to make sense of them, trying to remember.

"Jesus," he whispered, "I need your help again." The words left his lips with hardly a conscious thought.

Without knowing what he was doing, he began to recognize that groupings of black were separated by white spaces. Things like "j-e-l-l-o" and "a-p-p-l-e-s-a-u-c-e," "h-a-m," "s-c-r-a-m-b-l-e-d e-g-g-s," "o-a-t-m-e-a-l," "o-r-a-n-g-e j-u-i-c-e," and "t-o-a-s-t" danced in front of his eyes. But nothing clearly came to his mind. He had no memory, no frame of reference to enable him to understand the message of the words or associate anything with them. Suddenly, he remembered the words of the nurse, *Make a mark next to the food of your choice.*

He stared at the lines as he again picked up the pencil. Slowly, he began to move the grey point around some of the words. Some had repeating letters, such as *Jell-O*, *applesauce*, and *egg*. So he marked them. Still others had more than one group of black things on the same line. He thought they might represent a lot of food, so he marked *orange juice, iced tea, and hot chocolate.*

David looked at the paper. He moved his pencil over a few more items until he felt satisfied. He looked at his handiwork and smiled. God had helped him to accomplish this complicated task. "Thank you, Jesus," he whispered as he set the menu aside. The pencil dropped from his hands onto the tray, and he fell asleep, exhausted.

Later, when the hospital staff set trays of food before him, David's eyes widened. Plates and cups filled the trays. Colors and aromas danced in front of him, teasing him and tantalizing him. He bowed his head and silently thanked God, his Friend, for giving him this bounty.

David picked up the spoon. It ended up in the applesauce and slowly made its way to his mouth. The tang of the crushed apples pleased him and he savored the flavor, slowly letting the fruit slide down his throat. Each bite brought unexpected pleasure as he painstakingly relearned the taste, texture, and feel of food. With his senses marvelously responsive, David began to satisfy his hunger—bite by bite, chew by chew, swallow by swallow. He did not stop eating. Wasting the mountainous

Chapter Seven

amount of food was out of the question. Slower and slower, he continued to move his arm back and forth from plate to mouth until, finally, every bit of food was consumed. It had been a slow but steady effort, but David was satisfied—and he was exhausted.

Again, David fell asleep.

Later, he was awakened for his next meal. More trays laden with food surrounded him.

Without knowing what he had done, David had marked almost every item on the day's menu. For each meal he ended up with several entrees and a vast array of side dishes.

The doctors were still completely baffled by David's recovery. Consequently, they repeated all the tests that had previously been done in order to possibly find a changed variable. His room became a beehive of activity, with one intern after another studying this baffling case. Continuous examinations and tests were done in the hope of discovering what may have triggered David's recovery—or maybe even the possibility of learning what had caused the fever and delirium in the first place.

On the afternoon of October 18, David had a third lumbar puncture. As the needle was injected into David's spinal column, he was instantly aware of an intense pain sweeping through his body like a forest fire. He had never felt anything like it. His hair felt like it was on fire and his fingernails felt like they were going to split. His hands clenched in convulsion—unable to react, paralyzed by the pain.

The test seemed endless to David. Time moved one tortured breath at a time. Each swallow of air an ever-increasing battle in the war against the raging ocean of torment he was forced to endure. Throbbing, burning, unrelenting waves of pain washed over him and caught him in their violent ebb and flow. He lay completely drenched in sweat, incapacitated by the pain.

When the test was over and the needle removed, David was completely drained of energy. He lay on the table, motionless, and surrendered to the release of the moment. His eyes were closed, but he could hear the movement of the nurse's feet shuffling around the room while

Awakened

she finished the procedure. Finally, the nurse came to David and helped him back into an upright position.

As he was regaining his equilibrium, David achingly whispered, "I'm glad I only have to live through that once. I never want to do that again."

The nurse froze midmotion, her eyes opening wide. She blurted, "But, Mr. Anderson, I am sure this is not your first lumbar puncture. Let me see . . ." In disbelief, the nurse thumbed through David's chart. "Yes, this is your *third* spinal test."

The nurse, oblivious to David, continued, almost as if talking to herself, "I would think you would be accustomed to it by now."

David's face paled. The nurse's words penetrated his mind.

The feel of this excruciating pain was completely foreign. Nothing about it felt familiar to him, and yet the records showed his body had experienced it before.

The doctor who had been studying the preliminary results of David's test came back into the examination room. He took one look at the shade of David's face and assumed he was still suffering from aftershocks of pain from the test.

"How are you doing?" he asked as he stepped toward David, grabbing his arm and quickly taking his pulse.

David, confused and dazed, remained mute.

"The test went real well. We should be getting the results shortly." The doctor paused, waiting for some kind of communication from David.

There was none, so he continued.

"It's really quite miraculous, you know. The other times you had this test you were seemingly oblivious to the pain. You laid completely still, almost calm, as if you could feel nothing." The doctor chuckled ironically. "In fact, the evidence of pain you felt today was the most positive thing I have seen all week."

He smiled to underscore his last words. "You, Mr. Anderson, are a walking mystery; and you are one puzzle we hope to solve after we get a few more pieces of information. We need just a few more tests to help us unravel what's going on in your body."

At the thought of more tests, David began to cry. He wasn't sure how many more tests he could endure. He just wanted to go back to his hospital room and sleep. The doctor's words didn't seem important, nothing did. It was all too confusing.

Seeing David's tears, the doctor hesitated.

Chapter Seven

"It's OK, David, go ahead and cry. Anyone going through what you have been through deserves at least that much."

The tears welled up and came over David's cheekbones, coursing down his face.

"One day at a time," the doctor instructed, "and you'll get through this."

David grasped the doctor's hand, holding tightly. At least his face was a familiar one, something constant in this unfamiliar world of which he was now a part.

David was also subjected to a repeat electroencephalogram (EEG). He was led to a quiet, dimly lit room. The only furniture was an exam table and some foreign-looking machinery. There was a mirror in the room, but David stared blankly through his own reflection. All he saw was the mirror itself. Unknown to David, the wall of the room was a one-way mirror, the avenue for more intense, objective observation.

He was told to lie down on the table. Then, systematically, the technician began to place electrodes into his head. The probes penetrated his scalp to the surface of his brain to enable the cold machinery to record the electric currents developed in his brain.

David lay on the table, drenched with sweat, obediently subjecting himself to this torture. He knew no different. This was life. Finally, after what seemed an eternity, the test was ready to commence. The technician double-checked his work once more and gave his final instructions.

"David, all you need to do is just lie real still. We are going to record the activity in your brain, and we need your complete cooperation. We need you to be as quiet as possible." The technician smiled and patted David's arm. "Good luck," he said as he left the room.

David was alone. His head throbbed. He couldn't move. He could hear a soft ticking sound from somewhere in the room. He focused on it, but his mind could not identify it as a clock. Each breath was a new form of torture, the slight movement jarring the needlelike probes. Straining to keep his head immobile, he took a deep breath, hoping to calm himself. He felt the oxygen penetrate his lungs and then he slowly exhaled. His heart rate gradually slowed as he relaxed.

"OK, David," a voice boomed into the silent room, "we're ready to begin."

David's breathing stopped. He tried to locate the voice, pain seared into his skull as he strained to turn his head, his eyes frantically searching for the source of the sound.

Awakened

"You must lie as still as possible," the voice reprimanded, "or the test will be inaccurate."

David's breath slowly returned as he recognized one of the doctor's voices, even though he was totally mystified as to how the voice was sounding in the room. Slightly reassured, David tried to obey the command. He tried to not move.

His nose began to itch.

He wiggled his nostrils, vainly trying to relieve the discomfort. Unconsciously, his hand began to rise, responding to the insistent itch.

"Don't move, David," the voice arrested his action. "We need your complete cooperation."

David froze. He struggled to obey.

How long David laid there, he doesn't know. The ticking sound, the unidentified clock, went on and on. David lay with his eyes closed, focusing on the incessant pulse of the clock, trying to ignore all feeling in his body. The doctors spent as long as necessary to twist every knob on their machinery and record all brainwave activity needed to find the answers to their medical enigma: Why had David's condition suddenly improved?

The results came back. The doctors compared the findings to the data collected during a similar procedure performed on October 15. The final outcome: There was no explanation for the alteration in David's condition, but there was irrefutable, scientific evidence that a transformation had taken place.

> **The record is slightly abnormal, suggestive of a disturbance of brain function.... There is marked improvement since 10-15-65, especially in relation to the focal abnormalities, which have *completely disappeared* at present.**

A few days passed, and I stayed with David as much as possible. I continued to try to jar his memory, but it was like a huge eraser had been rubbed over his brain, leaving his memory blank. Yet, progress was being made. At each reference to our life together, David began to show more and more interest. I would bring up our girls in a conversation or point to one of the pictures I had left in his room, and he would reply.

Chapter Seven

He didn't respond with the usual sparkle I was accustomed to seeing from David before his illness, but at least he acknowledged my communication.

Bits and pieces of his remote memory were also returning. His gross motor skills were normal, even though he was very weak. He remembered how to write and even began to read a little. His comprehension still had much to be desired, but he was improving. He was starting to be more aware of what was going on around him.

On October 19, the day after David woke up, one doctor wrote:

> Patient is feeling much better but still has difficulty with memory and concentration. Mental state and orientation is improving slowly.

His communication skills were improving, although he had trouble remembering people's names. Everyone became "Doc." But, throughout the days, his vocabulary steadily increased. Sometimes he would talk to me. He would tell me what he had done during the day or to what test he had been subjected. Other times he remained silent, with words locked inside his head. He would listen to me without comment. Then he would yawn, the indicator I used to end my visit.

I was excited at the progress I was seeing. Any improvement was welcome. I was confident David would completely recover.

One doctor did not share my optimism. He wrote in David's chart:

> Patient continues afebrile [without fever] and stable. He complains occasionally of diffuse, poorly described headaches—no lateralizing. No neurological findings. *Recent memory is still deficient. Wife feels much improvement evident. I am less enthusiastic.* Problem still not clearly defined, though viral encephalitis most likely.

David slept. The doctors said sleepiness was a lingering symptom of his illness. This was definitely true. His chart is filled with comments like, "dozing long periods," and, "patient slept long intervals." He slept and ate and slept again—like a newborn baby.

David began to grow physically stronger. Soon he was able to sit up in bed regularly, and then later, to stand alone. The food he consumed began to rebuild his damaged body. By October 20, he was able to take short walks in the hall. David was feeling good, although a little weak. And he was having no difficulty talking or walking.

Awakened

By October 21, David had a good day. He was "up walking about in halls" with no overt weakness. He had "no difficulty maneuvering." He was "alert and his appetite was good." He offered "no special complaints."

As David grew stronger, the *No Visitors* sign came off his door. One of his friends remembers visiting him in the hospital. During their brief conversation, David confided to Bob the hospital was a really great place to live, adding, "There is even a cute girl who comes in and kisses me every day."

Bob was stunned. *Who but Joan would be kissing David? . . . Doesn't David remember his own wife?* Bob left the hospital keeping this conversation concealed for thirty years.

The stronger David became, the more obvious it was he would no longer need to stay under a doctor's constant care. He would be going home soon—but going home without his complete memory.

The doctors decided it would be wise for our children to visit their dad in the hospital before he was released. They realized that pictures of a ready-made family were nothing compared to real, living, breathing children.

The day dawned for the girls' expedition. I remember they were scared and nervous. They were excited about going to the hospital, but they were afraid of the germs there; maybe they would catch something. On top of those emotions, they were going to see their daddy again after over a week.

I was apprehensive myself because I wasn't sure how David would react to the girls. I also faced the hurdle of getting the girls through the encounter without revealing the full extent of David's condition. Would they find out their daddy didn't remember them?

David was nervous during their visit. He lay quietly on the bed, hesitantly smiling. Susan climbed on the bed, her blond locks swayed with her bouncing energy. Doreen and Donna stood close to the bed, quiet and respectful.

The visit was short but successful. No one cried and everyone smiled. Before leaving, the girls each hugged David and kissed his cheek. Then they walked quietly to the door.

Chapter Seven

Inside, my heart ached. Visions of many memories spanned before my mind's eye: the girls laughing and playing with David; hugs and kisses exchanged without any reserve; and the girls singing with strained vocal cords as David played the piano. These moments of our life I quickly buried in the recesses of my mind. I wanted to voice them to David but did not. I swallowed the lump that had risen in my throat, blinking my eyes to keep back my tears.

I smiled at David. I could see a faint sheen of perspiration on his brow, evidence of the stress our children's visit had placed on him. He saw my smile and responded in kind, a glimmer of trust flickered in his eyes. I reached out and touched his hand, he squeezed gently. *I love this man.* The sentiment burst from my heart. I blinked back the gathering moisture in my eyes, afraid to show too much emotion. I swallowed.

"I'll be back to see you later," I informed David of my plans. "You rest now."

David nodded, and I removed my hand. I walked to the door and left the room.

The girls' next stop on their hospital tour was the cafeteria. They relished the thrill of hospital food—on trays, no less! Their innocent excitement and energy communicated to me, touching me and lifting my spirits, and I thanked God for such wonderful children.

As test after test returned from the lab stamped *normal*, the doctors had no reason to keep David hospitalized. He was a healthy man of twenty-nine who was gaining strength every day. The doctors were baffled—doubly so because they had no logical explanation for David's awakening from delirium. They also had no scientific answer for the disappearance of his memory.

The diagnosis? The doctors reached no further conclusion than their working diagnosis of viral encephalitis: simply, "inflammation of the brain due to a virus." This generic tag gave a diagnosis, though a somewhat limited one. David's virus traveled into his brain and infected it, causing his brain to inflame. This is much more rare than the common viral complications, which might result in pneumonia or bronchitis.

Why was he better? The doctors didn't know.

Awakened

What happened to his memory and would it return? They didn't know. At this point, the doctors gave us hope with their statement, "David's memory should improve with time."

On Thursday, October 21, 1965, David was discharged from University Hospital. He was described as having "slight confusion now and otherwise normal."

The only instruction given to me was an order from the doctors to keep David inside. I was strongly urged not to allow him to go anywhere or do anything except return to the hospital for the follow-up examination in five days.

David's healing was evident. Every test result piling up in his file was normal. The virus was gone, but the doctors were still curious as to what it had been. Hoping to discover any remaining clues through follow-up testing, they let David go home.

Chapter Eight

The car slowly crept up the arterial. I braked to a halt, then swung to the left. I glanced at David to see his reaction to the car's movement. He had been sitting quietly in the front passenger seat since I had picked him up at the hospital. I had been trying to watch David as closely as I could during the fifteen-minute drive. I was hoping for some kind of reaction to his surroundings. He was so quiet, almost distant, it seemed as if he had withdrawn from everything. Perhaps the movement of traffic was too much for him to fathom. His overloaded brain and his thought processes had seemingly shut down.

I brought the Chevrolet into the carport and turned the key off. The last coughing spits from the car shook David out of his numbness, and he turned his head toward me. His eyes met mine for a minute then turned to stare out of the car window.

As my glance rested on him, I saw a flash of what looked like panic cross David's face. He began to break out in a cold sweat. I placed my hand on his arm, trying to reassure him and trying to communicate my concern and my love for him.

I scrambled out of the driver's seat, walked around the car and opened the door. The movement of the door being opened for him jarred David into motion, and he stepped out of the car. He was still weak from his days in bed. I took hold of his arm for reassurance—for myself as well as for him.

I was excited and scared. I was so glad David was back home, but I was apprehensive about how we were going to manage with his loss of memory. I wasn't sure exactly how extensive the memory loss was. The doctors had been somewhat vague. I felt in the dark as to what our lifestyle would be like. Would familiar things jar David's memory? Would he suddenly recall everything? Or would his past be lost to him forever?

We slowly made our way up the cement walkway—a walkway traveled hundreds of times by David in the past two years. It was one as familiar to me as it should have been to him. The apartment building we lived in had been built by David and his father. They had bought a small older home in order to remodel and enlarge the home for us to live in. Six more apartment units were built around the house to make a seven-unit building. David's parents lived in one of the other units. Every corner of this complex had been touched by David; even the cement walk we were on had been poured and finished by him. If there was anything tangible that would be more familiar to David, I was hard-pressed to find it.

I studied David. I witnessed every movement of his face, every thought reflected in his eyes. The little glimmer of hope that had sparked when I had thought about bringing David home to something familiar was slowly diminishing with every lack of reaction on his part. He stared impassively at everything he saw. No recognition, no emotion, no sudden burst of excitement with an enthusiastic "I remember this!" For me, it was growing disappointment.

With each step, I became more and more convinced that this "David" was seeing the shrubs, the evergreen tree, the apartment building, the stairs, and our front door for the first time. By the time we stood in front of apartment number 8, our home, drops of sweat were sliding down the side of David's face. His breathing was low and labored. His hands trembled slightly.

I inserted the key in the lock with a feeling of awkwardness. I remembered David doing this, David in charge—the man of the house. He had always been the one to open the door. I turned again to look at him and saw, as his gaze met mine, the fear of the unknown in his eyes. I could feel him calling to me for help, even though his lips were motionless.

I took his hand.

Chapter Seven

His palm was cold and clammy, so unlike the warm calloused hand I was used to. I stared at David, trying to read his emotions. I could sense his fear, but I knew there was more. Whatever he was experiencing was so intense I doubted I would ever be able to empathize with him. Inwardly, I groaned. How could I help him? How could I even begin to understand his thoughts, his feelings, his needs if I couldn't even begin to figure out what they were.

My inward musings were suddenly interrupted by the pounding of six feet running down the two flights of stairs that separated the girls from us. The girls had stayed with David's parents while I had gone to get David. They must have seen us walking alongside the building. Doreen, Donna, and a much slower little Susan, rounded the bottom stair to see us standing in our open doorway. At the sight of their father their smiles became beaming grins. One by one they made a beeline to my side while keeping all eyes glued on David. Susan grabbed my skirt and pulled, silently begging to be picked up. As I bent to do her bidding, Doreen, a polite eight-year-old, took the first plunge into conversation.

"Hi, Daddy," she whispered shyly.

David turned his eyes on her and smiled. Then, at her words, he turned his gaze back to the open door and the room beyond. He hesitated a brief moment, then walked through the door. The girls and I followed slowly behind, Doreen and Donna on either side of me and Susan in my arms. I placed Susan on the couch, and Doreen and Donna joined her. Quietly, we all waited and watched David.

I was apprehensive, wondering what the girl's reaction would be to having their dad home, but I needn't have worried. They behaved as if nothing was more important than having Daddy home again, even if Daddy was "still a little sick."

After standing motionless for what seemed like endless silent minutes, David began to slowly move about the living room. His eyes fleetingly lit on the treasures we had accumulated through ten years of marriage. I moved away from the girls to get closer to him, to offer my support if he wanted it. He slowly bent to pick up a small photograph, one of our family, but as his fingers touched the frame he snapped them away as if they were burnt.

I looked at his face. His eyes were wide with fear. He jerked his head away from me, trying to hide his emotion and moved to the other side

Awakened

of the room. I followed. I needed to be with him; I needed to somehow get close to him again, even if only with my physical presence.

David continued moving from room to room of our home. He left the living room, wandered through the dining room, and went to the kitchen. Our kitchen was long and narrow, with windows that looked out onto our backyard. At the window, he stood in silence, gazing at the motionless swing set and the playhouse he had built the girls. His eyes brushed mine. I will never forget the pain that seared into my soul with his look. His terror paralyzed me.

David restlessly moved down the hall, passing the stairway to the basement. He only glanced at the girls' room, then he continued down the hallway. He took a brief glimpse of the bathroom and our bedroom before completing his exploration. He turned and came, full circle, back to the living room. He stood helplessly in the middle of the room, looking completely exhausted. The emotions coursing through him had taken their toll. Dark circles stained the skin under his eyes. He looked haggard and forlorn. He was like a lost boy who was away from home for the first time—confused and frightened, not sure what to do or what to say.

I took an opportunity to depressurize the situation.

"Honey? . . ."

David's eyes immediately turned toward me at the sound of my voice, eager for a distraction from his fears.

"Would you like to lie down?"

Instant gratitude came to David's eyes. "Yes," he immediately answered.

Awkwardly, he started to turn, but his movement arrested in midmotion as he jerked to a stop. "Where do I go?" he tentatively questioned. His eyes blinked and met mine, blank and confused.

"How about lying down right here on the couch?" I suggested.

David looked at our girls, who quietly sat in expectant silence.

I motioned for them to get off the couch, and they immediately bounced to the other side of the room.

"Mommy," a single whisper came from the trio, "can we talk to Daddy?"

I turned around and saw the three, stair-stepped heads peering from the corner of the room, curiosity in each face. My heart melted at the sight of our daughters.

"Sure, but just for a minute, then Daddy is going to sleep for a while."

"OK," all three chimed together.

Chapter Seven

I waved them closer.

David was sitting on the edge of the couch now, still looking somewhat lost. His face softened as Doreen, Donna, and Susan slowly moved toward him, Doreen grasping Susan's small hand. Their gentle smiles and soft voices seemed to intrigue him, temporarily calming his shattered emotions.

As I looked at my reunited family, I thanked Jesus for bringing us together again. But my prayer of thanksgiving was interrupted by Donna's youthful voice telling her daddy that she was glad he was home. At the word *home*, David's face froze. Instantly, his serenity was replaced with stark fear, as if he knew that the word *home* implied something that concerned him, something expected of him, but he didn't quite know what it was.

I observed his immediate withdrawal and confusion and responded accordingly.

"Come on, girls, let's leave Daddy alone for now."

The girls obeyed me immediately, themselves sensing the change in David. They ushered themselves solemnly out of the room.

While covering David with a blanket, his eyes met mine. They were no longer confident, no longer direct. They now reflected emotions that were mostly absent in the David I had known. In his eyes I saw fear, confusion, and helplessness. He was uncomfortable with the girls. They were intruders into the safe little world he knew: a world of quiet, sterile hospital rooms and closed doors—a world without responsibility.

I quietly left the living room, leaving David to rest, and joined the girls in the kitchen.

"Mommy? When is Daddy going to be all better?" Doreen's small voice inquired. My heart cried out, but my mouth was silent. *Keep calm*, I told myself. *Jesus, help!* I silently pleaded. I said the first sane thing that came to mind.

"Jesus has already healed Daddy, but we just need to give Daddy some time to get used to being home again," I rationalized.

"OK."

She skipped off with her sisters to go to their room and play. As I watched them leave with their innocence intact, I continued.

"Lord, please help me. I want to help David, but I also need to have stability in this home for the girls. I don't know what to do." Tears wet my eyes. Silently, my heart cried out. *Oh, God! Where is David? Where is the man I married? My girls need their daddy back, but where is he?*

The begging halted as I summoned up words to express my loss. *I need David!* "Jesus. I need help!"

I could hear the girls in their room playing. I pulled myself together and bottled my emotions. *Later,* I told myself, *later, when you are alone, you can let your guard down—but not now.*

I walked farther into the kitchen; dinner needed to be made. Normalcy . . . yes, normalcy. That was what the girls needed, and that was what I was determined to give them, with God's help.

As soon as my dinner preparations were underway, I heard a soft tap on the front door and the slight squeak of the hinges as the door was opened. Simultaneously, a sugary-sweet "Yoo-hoo" shattered the quiet of our home. It was the voice of my mother-in-law. I dropped the utensils into the sink and rushed from the kitchen, wiping my hands on my apron on the way. I hoped to stop Helen from waking David. I stepped into the living room in time to see David's mother walking toward him. Increasing my pace, I stepped between mother and son.

"David is resting now," I whispered. "Would you mind coming back later?"

I could see a spark of irritation in her eyes so I rushed on, hoping to diffuse it.

"David is completely exhausted. The trip home from the hospital was very tiring. I am sure he would like to see you, though. Maybe after dinner when he is awake I can call you, then you can come for a visit."

I babbled on, hoping against hope to try to cool her down. Instead, my words aggravated the problem like water to a grease fire. She turned toward me, arched her back, then unleashed her tirade.

"You . . . you have no right whatsoever to tell me what I can or can not do regarding *my* son," she bellowed. With each word, her volume increased. Her eyes stared daggers into mine, bringing intense meaning to the phrase "If looks could kill." Her face flushed as she opened her mouth to continue.

"Please," I interrupted, "keep your voice down. Please, don't wake David."

My interruption made no effect except to incite her further.

Chapter Seven

"You are a wicked woman," she screamed. "You are manipulating my son, making him sick. And now you're even trying to keep me away from my son."

I stood with my mouth open and stared at her. I was dumbfounded at her accusation. I stood silent in the face of her indictment, realizing that my very presence in David's life was like salt on her wounds. I sighed and resigned myself to the undeserved verbal beating. Each word lashed through me, and I prayed that her torrent of abuse would be short-lived.

Then out of the corner of my eye, I saw David begin to stir.

"Please—" I urgently interjected, but she persisted.

"You waltz into my family and steal my son. Then you make him ill. And now you think you can keep him away from me—his own mother."

I winced as each word struck my ears, not knowing what to do.

David was waking up, disturbed by the loud, intrusive noise.

His gaze focused on the screaming, flushed stranger verbally attacking his gentle friend. He had never witnessed anything so frighteningly vicious, so cruel. Fear coursed through him, and the sound of her yelling grated across his senses. Every syllable, every nuance lashed through him and scratched over his nerves, fraying them ragged; and he began to shake.

I saw David's trembling begin. He turned his face to look directly at me, and his eyes were full of terror, confusion, and the beginnings of panic.

For the first time in our married life, keeping the peace with David's mother was not in David's best interest. Right now he needed quiet more than anything else—and absolutely no stress.

I knew I had to stand up to my mother-in-law. I knew David could not witness any more verbal abuse. And, regardless of my cowardice, I had to stop this woman.

I breathed a quick prayer for help and blurted, "Stop!"

My sudden burst momentarily stunned her into silence, and I jumped into the unexpected quiet.

"I ask you one more time—please leave now. You are upsetting David."

My words caused her to turn away from me and look at David. She took a step toward him, and he shrank back into the sofa cushions, cringing to distance himself from her.

Awakened

David's action did not go unnoticed. Her head swung around, her verbal onslaught in full swing once more.

"You are poisoning my son against me. I knew I should never have given permission to let you marry him. You are . . ."

As she ranted, I walked over to the door and opened it. I looked directly in her eyes, head held high, and quietly ordered her out of my home.

"I want you to leave. You are not welcome here right now. When you have calmed down, you may come back and see David, but not until he has rested. Now, please leave."

She opened her mouth and took a deep breath to continue.

"Now!" I repeated, my voice and tone commanding compliance.

Her mouth clamped shut, and she marched toward the open door. After she walked through the doorway, she turned toward me, her face flushed with anger.

"Well, I never . . . In all my life I never would have believed that . . ." she began.

I closed the door in her face.

I heard her gasp with stunned disbelief as the door clicked into place. Then I looked at my hand tightly grasping the doorknob. It was shaking. I lay my forehead against the door and closed my eyes, taking a deep breath. I was in shock and awe. I could feel my heart banging against my rib cage, racing with adrenaline. Gradually, it began to slow down, adjusting again to the quiet.

"Thank you, Lord, for getting her to walk through that door. I don't know what else I could have done to make her leave. Thank you, Jesus," I whispered.

I quickly put the chain on the door. A small shower of security rushed over me. It felt marvelous. I stood to my full height as I turned toward David. He was still shaken. His face was pale, and his eyes looked at me in wonder. My smile widened.

"Go back to sleep, honey. She's gone," I whispered.

His eyes began to droop, feeling safe once more. He visibly relaxed as if a blanket of peace had settled over him. Within moments, he was asleep again.

Sleep. This avenue of escape was David's gift from God. It seemed to repair his shattered emotions and give his mind rest from the tormenting emptiness that engulfed him.

Chapter Seven

I returned to the kitchen to finish my partially prepared meal.

The magnitude of creating normalcy out of the surrounding chaos completely boggled my mind. I didn't know what to do. David obviously craved peace and quiet, but the girls needed a normal father. I felt like I was caught outside on a dark, stormy night and my arms were aching from holding up a tattered umbrella to shelter my family.

―――

Later that night, the girls and David were in bed and the house was quiet. Dinner was over, baths had been given, and bedtime stories had been read. A surprisingly successful attempt had been made to have an average evening in our home. A small smile pushed at my lips. I was tired, but I felt a small sense of accomplishment. In the midst of the surrounding chaos we had found some order by meeting our mundane, everyday needs for just this one day. A seed of hope began to grow. If I could do this today, then, just maybe, I could do it tomorrow and the day after as well. It was a start.

My steps down the hall brought me closer to our bedroom. As I drew near the door, I heard something. I opened the door a crack, trying to see if David was all right. David was lying in bed, crying.

I heard the sobs coming from the other side of the room as I indecisively stood in the doorway. Should I go to David and offer my support? Maybe in some way my presence would help ease his sorrow, or maybe my expressions of love would only remind him of what was lost to him. Could my love and support make up for his twenty-nine forgotten years? I ached to touch David, to hold him.

My inadequacy stopped me.

I buried my head in my hands as I leaned against the door frame. My hair swept forward, shielding my view and muting the sounds coming from the bed. I didn't know what to do. What should I say? Could there possibly be a word or phrase that could even hope to turn around David's frailty of mind? I couldn't move.

Finally, the uneven sound of David's sobs penetrated my mind. They were no longer unintelligible groans, but his weeping was interspersed with words. I listened more intently. David was praying!

Awakened

The comfort this brought me was instantaneous. My breath left my lungs on a sigh of relief. David was not alone; he had Jesus, and he was praying for help—just as I had been. I backed away from the room. In my own strength, I was unable to help ease David's heartache, mainly because it was hard to see beyond my own distress. Yet, I knew with God's help I could face anything. And now David was tapping into that divine source as well. I knew our hearts belonged to Jesus and, with Jesus in control, our heartache and loneliness would ease.

We were two lonely people. I was missing my husband, and he was missing his memory. We were ships adrift in a savagely wild sea of confusion and loss. But in the quiet of my heart I heard a voice, *Take courage! It is I. Don't be afraid.* I recognized the words and the prevailing message from Mark 6:50 NIV. I could sense my Savior's presence in the midst of my raging storm. His voice soothed me and calmed the churning sea. My Deliverer was master of the storm in my life. *Peace, be still* rang out from my heart. The chill of the dark storm would pass. I was not alone, David was not alone.

The realization David was communicating with Jesus helped ease the pressure from my heart; I was no longer David's only support. Part of my despair had been the knowledge I was not enough for David, that he needed more strength than I could give him. But David knew where to find strength. The thought was comforting and freeing.

I walked into the living room and knelt down beside the couch. Now was the time. I could finally let down my guard and pour out my sorrow and confusion to God. I was finally alone and unobserved so I could be honest with my feelings. As I began to pray, I realized the oppressive emotions that had been so strong earlier had deserted me. Unexpectedly, I felt safe. The ache of my empty arms did not throb as they had only moments before when I had stood outside our bedroom door listening to David's cry. I could touch him with the arms of prayer. Miraculously, I found myself captivated by the goodness of God. Praise rose from the center of my being. "Jesus," the name sounded on my lips and reverberated through my heart. The majesty of His name overwhelmed me.

Both David and I had Jesus to help us, and that fact alone would bind us together. Jesus was our common ground, our link, a connecting thread stronger than any mutual experience could ever be. It tied us together and created a solid cornerstone upon which we could build.

Chapter Seven

That foundation would support us more securely than a million building blocks of memories.

I was awed, excited, and overcome by a fresh awareness of God's love for us. Before I even spoke His name He had begun to calm the raging storm in my soul. His name had stopped the lashing rain, and His words had brought peace to my heart.

Darkness had been victoriously banished with His light. God's love and protection astonished me, healing my emotions and calming my fears.

My mind settled on a well-known song. I whispered the comforting lyrics in the stillness of the night.

> Why should I feel discouraged,
> Why should the shadows come,
> Why should my heart be lonely,
> And long for heav'n and home,
> When Jesus is my portion?
> My constant friend is He;
> His eye is on the sparrow,
> And I know He watches me.
>
> "Let not your heart be troubled,"
> His tender word I hear,
> And resting on His goodness,
> I lose my doubts and fears;
> Tho' by the path He leadeth,
> But one step I may see;
> His eye is on the sparrow,
> And I know He watches me.
>
> I sing because I'm happy,
> I sing because I'm free.
> For His eye is on the sparrow,
> And I know He watches me. . . .

As the melody continued to flow from me, the lyrics struck a cord deep within my spirit. Those words were not mere religiosity, but the expression of an ageless, wondrous truth. In my mind I saw Jesus' face. His nail-scarred hands embraced me in protection and love, and His ever-constant gaze enfolded me, never losing focus. The encounter left

Awakened

me emotionally spent yet magnificently alive. Tears of joy streamed down my cheeks as the final verse of the hymn emerged from my heart.

> Whenever I am tempted,
> Whenever clouds arise,
> When song gives place to sighing,
> When hope within me dies,
> I draw the closer to Him,
> From care He sets me free;
> His eye is on the sparrow,
> And I know He cares for me.
>
> I sing because I'm happy,
> I sing because I'm free.
> For His eye is on the sparrow,
> And I know He watches me. [7]

Later, as I crept to bed, quietly trying to find my way in the darkness of the room, I listened for the sound of David's breathing. It was rhythmical and even, deep and healthy. He had obviously found rest and comfort and companionship through his prayers. I smiled because I had found the same. Laying down beside my sleeping husband, I immediately fell asleep.

Chapter Nine

The next morning I woke to the sound of music coming from my radio alarm clock. The lyrics of a well-known hymn proclaimed God's goodness, and spoke of his marvelous works.

The music and the words flowed through my soul and touched my heart with praise and thanksgiving. What a way to start the day! I reached for the alarm switch and turned the radio off, but the song of praise continued in my heart. Silently, not wanting to wake David, I continued my own private worship as I put on my robe and headed for the kitchen.

One by one the girls joined me. The girls and I ate together, then Doreen and Donna went off to school. Susan stayed with me. David had moved from the bed to the couch. He was exhausted after eating breakfast.

In the late morning I heard, once again, the all-too-familiar sound of our front door being opened, simultaneously with a light tap on the door. I had forgotten to rechain our front door after the girls left. My heart dropped. *Oh no,* I panicked. Only my in-laws had the nerve to walk in unannounced. With Susan on my heels, I ran to the living room. Sure enough, David's parents were standing by the couch, touching David's arm.

Awakened

Too late, I watched David stir and open his eyes. His face registered surprise and fright at the sight of his mother. But as his gaze rested on his father, he relaxed.

"Good mornin'," David's father drawled.

David just lay there.

"We wanted to come see how you are doing, Son," he persisted.

Neither one of my in-laws recognized my presence in the room, and I wasn't ready to draw attention to myself unless I had to intervene for David. I wasn't sure what kind of reaction I would get from David's mother.

After a few more unsuccessful attempts to elicit conversation from David, Eric switched tactics. He knelt beside his son and said, "David, I want to pray with you for the Lord to strengthen you and help you get back on your feet again real soon."

David nodded.

The two men closed their eyes in unison, and a father prayed for his son, straight from the heart. His Swedish accent thickened as emotion clogged Eric's throat, tears slipped past his tight eyelids and cascaded over his rugged cheeks. Praise to the healing Savior filled the room.

My mother-in-law stood next to the couch, lips stammering, eyes shut, and hands clasped.

Susan and I stood hand in hand. My own private praise to Jesus ascended silently while Susan watched everyone in awe.

David lay in peace and comfort, completely at home surrounded in God's presence. His face radiated with a glow, warming him from within.

As Eric's prayer ended, he stood up and grasped David's hand. "God be with you, Son." He turned and walked toward the door.

"Let's go, Mother, and leave David to rest."

Helen stood uncertain for a few moments; her face mirrored her indecision. Then she sighed.

"It's a great life if we don't weaken," she chimed as she followed her husband out the door.

I stood, mouth hanging open in amazement at her compliance. As the door clicked shut behind her, a small sigh of relief escaped my lips. Another miracle had just happened. Helen had visited and not said one hurtful word. Praise the Lord!

As this thought was crossing my mind, the door opened again. My heart jumped.

"I forgot I left this outside the door." Helen was standing in the doorway, a steaming pot in her hand and a smile on her face. At my questioning glance, she continued, "Some soup for your lunch."

She held the kettle toward me, her feet not stepping past the threshold, and I walked to her side. As I took the pot and thanked her, she smiled sincerely.

"We'll be down to visit again later," she concluded. She took command of the door and turned to leave.

"That would be nice," I said to the closing door. Amazingly, I meant the words.

I turned to check on David on my way to the kitchen with the soup. He was asleep again. I glanced down at the pot in my hands. It was as if our prior confrontation did not exist. God was again proving not only His faithfulness, but also His omnipotence in a seemingly hopeless situation with my mother-in-law. In awe at His hand in David's and my life, I sighed my thanks to God.

In the first few days after David's discharge from the hospital, our home life went through several major adjustments. David did nothing but sleep and eat; the girls and I tiptoed around him. We had no visitors besides family, and those were cut short because of David's fatigue. We never left the house. Sleep was all David wanted, sleep and solitude. He was not completely ready to face this foreign world into which he had been thrust.

Silence immediately became our way of life. David could stand no noise. No television, no record player, no loud noises at all could be tolerated. I was faced with the challenge of keeping three small children under the age of nine absolutely quiet. Our house became a quarantine of silence, interrupted only by infrequent hints of life. A small sliver of a smile or a softly spoken word of thanks from David became a source of joy to us.

During those few days, a few friends from our church brought food to our home. It was greatly appreciated because it helped relieve the strain of having to cook meals without making noise.

Awakened

David sat alone or slept. He was in a small world of his own—a place where no past or future existed. The day, the moment at hand, was all that mattered. He was polite but withdrawn. I often became overly solicitous, like an insecure child trying too hard to please. At times, I prayed for David to completely snap out of it so our life could begin to get back to normal. Sometimes I would glimpse a spark of what I thought was recognition or warmth in his eyes, and my hope and expectations would skyrocket. Then David would withdraw and crumble, dissolving into heart-rending sobs, calling out to God for help while I stood by helplessly, unable to meet his need.

In just the few days since David's release from the hospital, life had been stripped to its most basic form. The need of survival and the determination to recover some sort of normal routine became important. Everything else was swept away.

A few days after David had been home from the hospital, I ventured to give him a haircut. This was a novel experience for him but routine for me. I had been cutting his hair since we were married. The noise of the electric razor frightened David, but he trusted me enough to let me use it on his hair. He watched the process in a hand-held mirror.

Before I whisked the hair from David's neck, I brushed through the fresh crew cut with my fingers. It felt good to touch him.

I voiced my feelings, "You look great, honey. Your hair was getting so long I hardly recognized you." In the face of his silence I plowed on, trying to cover the awkwardness. "You look more like the David I know," I blundered.

David's head lifted at my words. His face paled.

I sucked in my breath at his reaction. My words bounced back to my own ears, condemning me.

"I mean—" I back-pedaled.

"It's OK, sweetheart," David interrupted. The color returned to his face as he forgave me.

David stood up, swaying slightly from the motion. Slowly he made his way back to the couch and a much-needed nap. He was exhausted from sitting up for so long.

Chapter Nine

I sighed and bit my tongue, cutting off a more elaborate apology. I wanted to beg David's forgiveness again and again while I kicked myself for my stupid remark. Yet I also knew I couldn't watch every word out of my mouth to avoid unintentionally offending him. I simply couldn't live that way. I swallowed. We definitely had some major adjustments to make.

"Lord, help, . . . please!" I whispered as I cleaned up the hair clippings from the kitchen floor.

Once everything was picked up and put away, I went to check on David. He was sleeping like a baby, peacefully and at rest. I looked at his face. He was pale and gaunt from his mandatory "Indoors only" order from the doctor, but I also noticed other changes. The energetic vitality that had almost burst from David only six weeks earlier had disappeared. He was like . . . like an empty shell. The personality of the man I had married was lost, and I had not yet found the new one. I faced the greatest obstacle of my life—to discover the essential nature of the person to whom I was married.

On October 26, five days after David's release from the hospital, we returned to the hospital for his first follow-up examination. I was able to borrow David's parent's car and get a baby-sitter for Susan. I bundled up David and led him to the vehicle.

I saw a flash of recognition in David's eyes as he stated, "This is the car that brought us here."

David remembered the car and he remembered the hospital. Apparently, new memories had been formed and were now being recalled. This thought lifted my spirit as I drove to the clinic. David was no longer completely without a past; he had memories, albeit just a few.

I pulled into a parking stall and turned the ignition key. As I glanced at David, his face lit briefly with a bright smile. I was stunned. It had been so long since I had seen his smile that I had forgotten how moving it could be. It was reminiscent of the man I had married, and it warmed my heart. I smiled back, communicating my love. David's lack of withdrawal encouraged me. Pressing this small advantage, I reached my hand to touch him.

Our fingers met, sparking a flood of memories in my mind. We walked hand in hand into the doctor's office and sat down. We waited.

When we were finally called into the exam room, the doctor was looking over a chart I presumed to be David's. We sat and waited for him to look up. He raised his eyes and his gaze swept past me to focus directly on David. Immediately, his eyes swung back to me, piercing in their intensity.

"I thought I told you to keep David at home." His eyes nailed me to my chair, accusing and derogatory. His tone belittled me as if I was a naughty, disobedient child.

I was stunned.

His scathing remarks continued.

"Don't you realize the importance of David's rest?"

"But—" I interjected, unclear as to why I was receiving this scolding. My astonished sputter was ignored.

"David needs to build up his strength, not go gallivanting around town to visit every bank and barber, no matter how urgent." The doctor's nostrils flared with irritation and a slight flush brushed his features. "Can't I trust you to do what is best for David? Can't you follow simple instructions?"

His verbal spanking complete, he stopped ranting, but the accusations remained in his eyes and there they simmered.

The word *barber* flashed in my head. The haircut! I had given David a haircut, and the doctor thought I had brought David to a barber.

A protest rose from my gut over this injustice, but I pressed my lips together, refusing to give in to the anger. Trying to remain calm, I took a deep breath.

"Excuse me, sir," I swallowed and cleared my throat, "David has been nowhere except home and now, here." I paused, letting my words register with him.

I saw the intensity blaze in the doctor's unbelieving eyes. I continued my defense before he could muster a new attack.

"I cut David's hair myself—at *home*," I emphasized.

At my words, the doctor briefly paled. The previous flame of outrage was immediately extinguished. He blinked his eyes from the dousing. Choking out an embarrassed "Oh," he dropped his eyes. Then the doctor consulted his chart, flipping through the pages to regroup his thoughts and turned to David.

David sat nervously sweating from the tension in the room. He was unsure about what was happening. His gaze swung from the doctor to

Chapter Nine

me, confusion and apprehension filtering through his eyes. Childlike, his hand fumbled with the arm of his chair, seeking any kind of security he could find.

Hoping to reassure him, I smiled.

Satisfied, his eyes turned back to the offensive doctor.

The doctor saw David's reaction to his chastisement of me and tried to make David more comfortable, himself shifting with embarrassment in his chair.

"Well, David," the doctor chuckled, trying to diffuse the tension. "I think you have a good, little wife here." He cleared his throat again, his eyes never glancing in my direction.

"She seems to be taking good care of you." He smiled at David, and David responded.

The doctor dismissed his blunder and professionalized the visit. "Let's take a closer look at you then, shall we?"

David relaxed and nodded his head.

The results of the examination and follow-up tests were normal. David was completely healthy in every way. But there was still no scientific explanation of why his memory had not yet fully returned. The doctor wrote in David's chart:

> Patient normal including vital signs, fundi, and neurology. . . . Memory still hazy but better. Patient more nervous.

The doctor wrote a prescription for tranquilizers to help soothe David's nerves—but just being out of the company of this particular doctor also calmed David. We were sent home with "more time" prescribed as the remedy to fix David's amnesia. Another follow-up appointment was scheduled for a week later, November 2.

During the next week we remained at home, and David continued to get stronger. He was able to sit up for longer periods of time. At times, David still seemed to exist in his own little world, but I noticed he was becoming more comfortable talking and interacting with me and the girls. I felt good about those changes. David seemed to be improving.

November 2 arrived, and David was examined again. A different doctor wrote in his chart:

> Patient returns today with *very little change in memory.* Converses better and more alert. More appropriate responses. Wife thinks he is

> slightly better. He is more nervous. He is *unable to recognize friends,* etc. I am somewhat surprised at such slow recovery. Return in one week.

At home, a few friends visited us. David still did not remember any of them, but, with my help, he was able to talk with them for short periods of time. He continued to sleep a lot, but, when awake, he was up and walking around the house. His physical condition continued to improve.

One week later, David had a third follow-up examination. On November 9, the doctor wrote:

> Patient returns today better able to cope with daily activities and interject himself socially. Neurological exam revealed only slight change down in a small 1 x 1 cm area. He is improving. Return in two weeks.

By November 23, David was still taking tranquilizers. He was very nervous, and I continued to hear him occasionally crying. Shedding tears was one way he relieved the overwhelming stress he faced each day.

Simple things were strange and drew unexpected responses. On rare occasions, we would turn on the television. David would have an eerie, paramnesia-type experience, as if he had seen the show before. Even live shows, such as a news broadcast, seemed familiar to him. It made me wonder just how close David had been to eternity. Had he partially seen a record of life events unrooted in time? Or were the tranquilizers messing him up?

At his fourth follow-up visit, David was again described by the doctor:

> Patient continues to improve in mental status. *Still nervous.* Return in three weeks.

By the time David's final examination arrived on December 14, he was beginning to adjust to his life with limited memory. He had stopped taking the tranquilizers because his nerves were stabilizing on their own. But even without the influence of the tranquilizing drug, David continued to experience the discomfiting, unpleasantly familiar *deja vu* when watching television. To cope with this phenomenon, we left the TV off.

David was physically becoming stronger and stronger, but at times he experienced severe headaches. Noise was the catalyst for them, so

Chapter Nine

our family continued in our silent lifestyle. The girls played in whispers, discipline was done with a look, and walking on tiptoe was a perfected art.

The mysterious odors continued periodically to reek in David's head. The doctors believed the offensive odor was a lingering symptom of his virus that would fade with time.

The result of David's final checkup had a familiar ring:

> Patient has noted further improvement both in mental performance and physical strength. He has not required any sedation lately. Physical exam unremarkable. No need for further follow-up.

Time. All would be well in time.

The University of Washington doctors closed David's file with a letter to Dr. Lehmann.

> Dear Doctor Lehmann:
> This was a very interesting problem in diagnosis of a potentially very serious disease. I am most pleased that Mr. Anderson improved so rapidly.
> By October 27, his . . . memory was still "foggy." There are no results yet on our viral studies. . . . In any event, he is making an uneventful recovery.
>
> Sincerely,
> Attending Physician

When Dr. Lehmann received this correspondence, he went to his file cabinet. There he found his records for David. With a bold hand, he scrawled the word *miracle* across the bottom of the paper. He inserted the letter into the file.

The medical case of David Anderson was closed.

Chapter Ten

The nights were cold, the days were gray and misty, and rain touched the streets of Seattle at least once a day. Christmas was fast approaching. Since leaving the hospital, David had been out of the house only to go to the doctor. He was always fatigued.

David lived in his own world of perpetual discovery. New sights, sounds, and smells constantly intruded into his senses. Sometimes he calmly accepted them into his life; other times he shut them out, refusing to embrace the new sensations, and he would retreat into a world of incredible confusion.

For the most part, David had not been around people except for myself and the girls, his parents, and a few close friends. Even those social visits were awkward and exhausting. With the holidays so close, I was becoming more and more concerned about David's ability to cope with any of the usual festive activities and all of the people who came with them. Would he be able to handle the well-meant good cheer expressed by everyone? Could he handle the strange sights and sounds—and the noise? I didn't know. Would people understand David's unresponsiveness? Would they be offended, or would they even notice?

Almost everyone wanted to believe David was completely well. If they talked about David's amnesia at all, it was either mentioned and

Awakened

then forgotten, or it was dismissed out of hand as being too farfetched. Most of our acquaintances were Christians and, as such, were willing to accept the simple explanation of David's miraculous healing—end of story! Some wanted to pat David on the back and breathe a sigh of relief that they didn't have to worry about him anymore. Others were initially understanding of David, but when he wasn't completely back on his feet in good time, the situation grew too awkward. It was simply too uncomfortable to reenter the world of a man who no longer remembered them. Many chose to avoid this problem by quietly fading out of our lives.

Even David's family refused to believe David had a memory problem. To make matters worse, Helen blamed me for David's condition. To her, David acted differently.

He *was* different.

Instead of accepting David's amnesia, Helen accused me of "poisoning her son's mind" against her. So I continually received sharp looks and cutting remarks meant to revenge her son's altered personality. I did my best to ignore her.

David seemed oblivious to the dismantling of our social life.

I began to feel more and more isolated and burdened. At times, I became resentful at the insensitivity of others. Then I would feel guilty at my uncharitable thoughts toward them. Still, the responsibility of David's recovery lay with me—from performing menial tasks to being the sole emotional support David desperately needed.

But there were times when I lost patience with my role as the constant giver. I was Joan the decision maker, Joan the mother, Joan the encourager and comforter, Joan the rock upon whom everyone leaned. No one seemed to know how exhausting it was to be a rock. It was a gigantic effort just to stand firm.

At times, the monumental weight of this responsibility pressed on me until I felt almost crushed. Life had taken an unexpected turn, leaving me painfully off balance. There were no longer clear-cut definitions in the leadership roles of our family.

The questions W*ho is David?* and *Who am I?* and W*hy did God heal David's physical body leaving his mind in confusion?* spun in my mind. They bombarded me, bringing confusing and disturbing implications.

I tried to keep up the victorious front I thought everyone expected of me and would approve of, but periodically the façade would crumble. Usually at night, when everyone else was in bed, I would fall on my

Chapter Ten

knees and cry. One night, I broke. Shattered and alone, and I cried out to the only One who knew I needed help.

"Oh, God," I cried. "I can't carry this alone. I need help."

I felt locked in a prison of isolation and loneliness. No one understood my agony of seeing the face of the man I loved without really recognizing or knowing him.

As I knelt, faces of friends and family who could potentially help me flashed through my mind. One by one they were erased off my mental list. Some were too busy with families of their own, some lived too far away to be of help, and still others were convinced David was completely healed and "all was well." There were a small few who had been supportive during David's hospital stay, but I knew the kind of help I needed wasn't available from them.

My hands cradled my head as tears followed a well-used path over the contour of my face. I desperately needed to be touched on a personal level. If only someone would grab me by the shoulders and say, "Joan, you're doing a good job, and I see the extra burden you carry," and, "It's all right to hurt and grieve for your loss. Don't feel guilty." But I sat, seemingly abandoned, my fragile humanity exposed to devastating waves of guilt, drowning in feelings of isolation.

I picked up my Bible and opened the soft leather cover. I knew the words printed in black and white before my eyes were more real, more dependable and steadfast than any feeling or emotion I could ever experience.

I had reached into the deepest part of myself for answers and came up empty handed. So I reached beyond myself. I did the only thing I *could* do. I directed my questions and uncertainties to the One who had the answers.

"Jesus, I don't know why I am feeling the things I am. I feel pressed in from all sides, with no where to go. I feel crushed beneath this weight." I hesitated, uncertain of how to express my anguished thoughts. "I know Your Word is true, but, oh, God, I am not experiencing the reality of Your Word. I need You to make Your Word a reality in my life."

I sobbed out the next words, "God, I feel so oppressed. . . . Please, somehow show me Your Word is true. Show me I am not carrying my burden alone. . . . Help me to place this load on Your shoulders and not to try to carry it myself. Help me to continually believe in You."

Awakened

The tears coursed down my face, cleansing and healing me as they fell. From somewhere in my subconscious the entreaty, *In everything give thanks . . . for this is the will of God for you*, floated into my consciousness. I didn't feel like thanking God. Nothing in my immediate circumstances motivated me to praise Jesus, yet the words *in everything* required obedience.

After making a deliberate decision to obey God's Word, I stood from my deflated position and lifted my hands toward heaven. My hands felt like lead, but I kept them up out of shear determination. I opened my mouth to speak, but my tongue refused to move. So, silently, I began to think words of praise to Jesus, and slowly the silent praise and thanksgiving to my God loosened my tongue.

"Thank you, Jesus. Thank you for being true and faithful, even in the face of my doubts and fears." The words poured from the depths of my being, words of faith, words of trust.

"I believe in You. I believe in Your Word, even in the face of my conflicting emotions. . . . I will praise You, regardless of my feelings."

As the words spilled out of my mouth, a song rose from my heart and burst from my lips.

> When you're up against a struggle
> That shatters all your dreams,
> And your hopes have been cruelly crushed
> By Satan's manifested scheme.
> And you feel the urge within you, to submit to earthly fears,
> Don't let the faith you're standing in, seem to disappear.
>
> Praise the Lord!
> He can work through those who praise Him.
> Praise the Lord, for our God inhabits praise.
> Praise the Lord, for the chains that seem to bind you,
> Serve only to remind you,
> That they drop powerless behind you,
> When you praise Him. [8]

The song lifted my heart, the burden was lighter. Suddenly I realized that no longer was my praise and thanksgiving a product of a cold decision, but it was spontaneously pouring from within me. I was experiencing true worship and praise, and a genuine transformation had taken

Chapter Ten

place in my heart. Praise to Jesus had brought about a change in my emotions. My transitory feelings had come under the power and authority of Almighty God through my praise to Him.

The next day, the doorbell rang.

I went to the door and opened it, and standing in front of me was a large, dark-haired man. It was Walter Buck, the new senior pastor of our church, Evangel Temple.

His face was kind though somewhat pale. His eyes were sunken and accentuated by dark circles, yet they held compassion and something else—something that looked almost like understanding. The lines and ridges etched in his face confirmed that he was still recovering from his recent heart attack. His gaze held mine confidently, and it held a spark of health and hope.

He smiled at me as he spoke, "Hello, Joan. I hope I have not caught you at a bad time. I just felt like I should come see you and David this morning."

His sensitive smile warmed my heart, and his words pierced through my loneliness. I held the door open wider for him to enter our home.

"Please, come in. I am so glad you came." My voice rang with sincerity as I welcomed him.

"How are you feeling?" I asked, genuinely interested in his answer.

He smiled appreciatively at my concern.

"I'm doing quite well as long as I take things slow. The Lord has helped me every step, and I'm even finding more time to be on my knees praying. The things that were so important before my heart attack aren't so important now." The pitch of his voice dropped slightly at his admission. "Ill health tends to rearrange your priorities."

I nodded and agreed, "I understand."

"I'm sure you do," he acknowledged.

He continued, "I am here because I would like to spend some time praying with David, and maybe keep him company. You may join us, or if you would like, maybe I could be with David and then you would be free to do some of the things you need to that perhaps are being neglected because of your care for David."

Awakened

Tears welled in my eyes. I could hardly believe the impact this little thoughtfulness had on me. My insides went weak when offered this compassion and understanding. I choked out an affirmative reply and shakily led the way to David.

David responded positively to Pastor Buck. The two of them bonded through their mutual need for and reliance on God. They stayed in the living room, cloistered together in prayer for an hour. Every time I walked by the room, I heard their voices blending together in an atmosphere of petition and praise. The presence of Jesus filled the room, and both men drew strength from their Redeemer and Healer.

When Pastor Buck got up to leave, I walked him to the door.

"Thank you for opening your home to me," he simply stated. "Your home is blessed. Jesus lives here, and David is hand in hand with God."

He smiled as he continued. "I came to help and encourage him; instead, my spirit has been renewed. I came to give and found myself receiving."

His face shone as he said those words. The lines of fatigue and pain were not as noticeable as they had been before. An inner peace radiated from his spirit and smoothed his features, softening the signs of pain and suffering. It was as if all that had gone before had been greatly diminished. He had been in communion with Almighty God, and God's touch had comforted and soothed him.

Pastor Buck walked through the door with another heartfelt "thank you" and a promise to come again tomorrow.

I was again moved to tears as I realized God had answered my prayer for help. I leaned against the closed door, amazed. The wonder of Almighty God's direction in the life of mere man, touched my heart. I turned away from the door, wanting to see David's reaction to Pastor Buck's visit. I hoped it had not been too much for him.

As I looked at David, I realized I had no need to worry. The same peace and serenity that had been visibly present with Pastor Buck was magnified twofold on David. Emotions I had not seen since before his illness were now expressed on David's countenance—emotions like security and complete trust. He was content and even happy.

He smiled at me. It was a genuine I'm-glad-to-see-you kind of smile. His eyes were clear, and they sparkled as he looked directly at me. His directness and responsiveness left me speechless.

Chapter Ten

"That was a nice man. I hope he comes again."

As the words left his lips, David yawned. His spirit was renewed by God's presence, but his body was physically exhausted.

"Pastor Buck said he would try to come again tomorrow. Now, I think you should try to get some rest."

David's expression changed at my words. His brow furrowed as he searched his frustratingly blank mind. He asked the question that was bothering him. "When is tomorrow?"

Dumbfounded, I stared at him. *Is he kidding?*

His eyes stared back at me with candor as he patiently waited for my response. He had asked the question in honest sincerity. He really did not know what the word *tomorrow* represented.

Trying to hide my dismay, I answered him like I had answered similar questions from my children—straightforward and simple.

"It will get dark soon. . . ."

His brow cleared.

"Then we will go to bed."

He nodded in understanding.

"When we wake up in the morning, it will be tomorrow." His eyes registered comprehension. He nodded slightly as his eyes began to droop. The strain of hard concentration needed to end. David fell asleep.

This first visit was one of many from Pastor Buck. Often he would show up on our doorstep and I would usher him in to see David. Then, after visiting for a few minutes, I would leave the two men alone to pray. They ministered to each other in prayer, each one drawing strength from their communion with Christ.

I firmly believe this daily contact with God enabled David to have the strength and the courage to face the world outside the walls of our home. I also believe Walter Buck's friendship with David was the beginning of a new life for him. David had found a friend with the same interests and desires, someone interested in nothing but talking with Jesus.

As each day passed, David became more and more eager for the pastor's visit. He was slowly breaking out of the shell into which his amnesia had put him.

Pastor Buck himself grew stronger as each day passed. He began to pick up more and more of the load of his responsibilities as a new pastor. He also began to realize he was going to need assistance. In David,

Awakened

Pastor Buck saw potential help. David lived his faith, and David walked in total dependence and trust in God.

~~~

We chose to have a very quiet Christmas, and we were able to get through the holiday season without incident. David stayed home, and a few friends and family came to visit us.

A new year, 1966, was ushered in, and Pastor Buck still came to pray. Slowly, David continued his courageous effort to try to understand what was going on around him. He had become more accustomed to our home and the girls. The girls had a wonderful way of accepting David just as he was, without pointing out his flaws and weaknesses. They did not make demands on him or expect more from him than he was able to give. He even, in time, began to find his soft, quiet conversations with them enjoyable. He especially related to Susan, who was only two. Susan's young mind and David's budding memory developed together. Simultaneously, they learned to distinguish between likes and dislikes, and they played together—even building a snowman in the backyard.

Each day David grew stronger.

Experimentation and learning became David's agenda for each day, and each discovery led to more and more questions—and sometimes confusion. Rarely did David initially experience real understanding of what was going on, but, bravely, he continued to strive and grow.

David and Susan building a snowman—1966

One day David experimented with the baby grand piano standing in our living room. This instrument had always been an integral part of our home. During the ten years of our marriage, David had actively pursued his various interests in music, and playing the piano had been an important part of his daily life. But since the hospitalization, the piano had been silent. Things had been so confusing that I really hadn't noticed the absence of its sound, until the day David's curiosity got the better of him.

David had a feeling of being drawn to the three-legged piece of furniture. He found himself seated in front of the instrument. It was *beautiful!* A row of white and black pattern surrounded by rich brown wood. It was aching to be touched . . . calling to him. Yet, David didn't *know* what to do.

He sat for a minute admiring the shiny smooth surface and the contour of the wood. Slowly, he raised his hands to gently touch the glossy white rectangles. They felt good. His fingers automatically cupped and fell into a triad position. He pressed down and—a wonderful sound emerged! Surprised, he jerked his hands off the keys.

His heart was pounding! He was excited at his discovery.

He brought his hands down again, and his fingers began to move of their own accord. He sat there, in awe at the harmonious melody his hands were making.

I was in the kitchen at the time this happened. I heard a perfect chord struck, then quickly released. A short span of silence followed. Then a beautiful melody began to fill the air. A familiar classical piece of music danced through the corners of each room and gently filled our home.

I dropped what I was doing, immediately drawn toward the music. It sounded like David's playing, but it couldn't be! *Could it?*

The music continued to flow perfectly as I rounded the corner to the living room. Sure enough, David was sitting at the keyboard in pure enjoyment. I looked at his face. An awestruck expression covered his features, and he was slightly flushed with excitement. His wondrously bright eyes were staring at his moving hands, disbelief mixed with delight in his gaze. I didn't interrupt David and just listened to him play. As each note sounded, I recognized the melody. It was a classical piece David had memorized while taking piano lessons as a child.

I looked at his hands. They moved effortlessly and unerringly over the keyboard, as if they were destined to create music. They stroked the keys, touching here and gliding there. They were masters at what they were doing.

The notes danced vibrantly in the air. I stood transfixed by the melody and the musician. David was animated, seemingly plugged into some unseen power.

Awakened

His hands responded. His foot responded. It pressed down, sustaining the harmony. Then it lifted, muting the sound in preparation for a new chord. Then down again to blend the vibrations once more.

Finally the melody came to an end, and David stopped playing. He sat quite still, unaware of anything but the lingering tones vibrating in the air. He had a wonderfully captivated look on his face. It wasn't until the last echoes disappeared that he turned toward me.

I saw the irrepressible sparkle in his eyes, a light I had not seen for quite some time. I swallowed, hesitant to speak but too moved to remain silent.

"That was beautiful," I whispered, afraid to break the enchantment of the moment.

He stared at me, still mesmerized by the melody his hands had created.

"How . . . how did you play?" I questioned.

He shook his head.

His eyes dropped to the piano keys, his fingers affectionately stroking the ivory.

"I-I don't know," he stuttered, "I just sat down and . . . and the music came out of my hands."

He lifted his hands and turned them over, inspecting each finger, looking for some sort of sign, some clue, some unseen switch that would explain what had just happened.

I couldn't believe my ears. *What is happening? Are David's hands remembering things his head did not? Is that possible?*

David's hands moved onto the keys once again.

"I don't know," he mumbled again as he stroked the keys and the fresh melody of one of David's favorite songs filled the room.

The musical lyrics spoke about the Savior coming in a dream; taking our hand, and speaking our name.

David closed his eyes as his hands created the music. I could see his lips begin to move in praise to Jesus, thanking him for this gift.

I tiptoed out of the room. Yes, David had the right approach. It didn't matter how or why he was able to play the piano. All that mattered was God had blessed David with the gift of expression.

From that day on, David used his gift. Whenever he would get depressed or upset at his lack of memory or physical weakness, he would sit at the piano and play. His hands never let him down. The muscles of

Chapter Ten

his fingers remembered how to touch the keys and which notes to play together. And every time, he produced beautiful music.

David shared the experience with Pastor Buck, and it generated an even greater desire in Pastor Buck's heart for David to become involved in the church. He kept praying and waiting for God's timing in the matter.

Chapter Eleven

The most courageous thing David did during the first few months after he "woke up" was take a trip to our church. It was the first time David had been outside of our home, with the exception of his follow-up examinations at the University of Washington Hospital. Every day he had been getting physically stronger, and his ability to play the piano had bolstered his confidence; so both of us felt it was time for him to venture out.

On that particular Sunday, with all three girls piled in the back seat of my father-in-law's car, and David in the front passenger seat, I drove to church.

As I pulled the car into the parking lot of Evangel Temple, I could feel the tension radiating from David. I glanced briefly at his profile. His jaw was clenched, and I could see his pulse rapidly beating out a reckless rhythm. My eyes dropped to his hands. They were fisted and motionless, held in a tight protective grip in front of him in a vain attempt to defend himself from what his eyes were seeing.

I looked to see what David was viewing: Happy churchgoers in their Sunday attire were dotting the driveway and parking lot—mingling, laughing, and chatting about the weekly news. They were oblivious to the tension building in our car.

Awakened

I pulled the car into a parking space and turned off the ignition. The girls sat quietly in the back, not saying a word. I turned to David again and reached for his clenched hands. As our fingers touched, he flinched, but I didn't pull back. I knew he was frightened and nervous, yet I also knew he needed my touch.

"David," I whispered.

He turned his head toward the sound of my voice, dragging his eyes away from the scene observed through the car window. His eyes met mine, and I could clearly see the fear and apprehension this man felt. His hands began to tremble. A slight sheen of perspiration broke out on his forehead, and his breathing accelerated. His mouth dropped open to breathe quicker as his anxiety escalated.

I tightened my fingers over his slightly clammy skin in an attempt to reassure him.

I rapidly whispered, "Girls, let's pray for Daddy."

David's eyes pierced through me in desperation and gratitude as he nodded. We bowed our heads.

"Jesus, help David. Help all of us today. We need Your strength to make it through this service. After all, we are here to worship You."

At my words, the tension began to recede from David's hands. The presence of Jesus, so strong around us, filled the car. I ended my prayer with, "Thank you, Jesus. Amen."

From the back seat, three small voices echoed: "Amen."

David relaxed in the seat. His only words were, "Thank you."

I looked at him, expecting him to say more, but his eyes were closed. He was inwardly talking to his Best Friend. Jesus was strengthening him and giving him peace.

I pulled the keys from the ignition and dropped them into my purse. I opened the door and held back the front seat for the girls to exit as well. After closing my door, I went around the car to open David's. He sat and waited for me. I tried to open his door, but it was locked. David just looked at me. I sighed, and instead of trying to explain what I needed, I retrieved the keys and unlocked the door myself. David just sat there, patiently waiting for me to go through whatever was necessary to get him out of the vehicle. Finally, he stepped out, and I took his arm.

I looked at David in his three-piece, dark blue, pinstripe suit. He looked great. "You look very nice today," I said, attempting to distract David. David smiled weakly at my words, but said nothing.

Chapter Eleven

Suddenly, I felt his arm stiffen. My eyes looked in the same direction as David's. We both saw our friend, Cliff, coming toward us. I felt David trembling again. The slight shaking radiated through his arm to my hand, but David remained mute. Without conscious thought or prior strategy, I did what I could to help. Immediately, I fell into the role of secret informant. I turned my head slightly to aim my words at his ear; the facts left my mouth in a whisper.

"The man coming toward us now is Cliff," I prompted. "You have known him all your life, and he is a good friend."

As Cliff's steps brought him face to face with David, he extended his hand. I pushed David's arm slightly forward, and David responded correctly by moving with me. Cliff grasped David's hand and pumped it up and down, saying, "Hi, Dave! You look great. How are you feeling?"

The men dropped their hands, and David responded.

"Hi, Cliff—"

"It is sure nice to have you back," Cliff broke in. "I've got to run now; I'm teaching Sunday school. I'm sure I'll see you later."

He left us with a smile and a salute.

David sighed. He was visibly taxed by the swiftness of the conversation, but he was also relieved. His first personal encounter was over, and, without rehearsal, he had successfully performed while following me—his offstage prompter. I squeezed his arm, and we walked into the sanctuary.

The rest of the morning went just as smoothly. Before David met anyone, I was able to cue him as to the person's identity. David was able to meet everyone with a smile and their name on his lips.

I was proud of how well David carried himself that day, and I was even a little proud of myself. We had pulled it off. David had gone to church without making any embarrassing scenes. We had created no problems. We had been able to sit and enjoy the atmosphere in the service with only minimal explanations. I felt wonderful, happy with our achievement.

The one major factor I did not realize at that time was the mistaken impression that day would leave behind us. David's wonderful "success" planted seeds of distorted truth which would grow into gross misconceptions and unrealistic expectations. The general opinion of our church family and friends was that David was fine, maybe a little weak and a little quiet and forlorn but generally healthy. And certainly, they thought, the little changes that were visible with David would resolve over time. The general belief was David would soon be "back on his feet again."

As time moved on, I began to realize more and more how hard that misconception would be on David and me. As days, weeks, months, and even years passed, people expected more of David than he was able to give. They wanted and expected him to remember the past—and remembering was the one thing David could not do. Any impression of David recalling the past was either due to prompting from me or David's remembering what he had learned since his recovery.

My role as secret informant had created a permanent need for my services to David. More and more, David relied on me to supply the answers to the void in his mind; and the more I secretly cued him, the more the façade of an undamaged memory emerged. The image of a healthy man, physically strong and mentally sound, became established with many of our acquaintances.

One person not fooled by this well-intentioned falseness was Pastor Buck.

David's slow recovery brought on another problem. He had been out of work for about half a year, so we had no income. David's parents periodically asked if I needed financial help, but I didn't want to become more indebted to them. We were already living in their apartment building and driving their car. I didn't want to start taking money as well.

One option was for me to get a job. There were so many complications involved with my becoming employed that it was hard to even consider this possibility. But I knew, as each day went by, I would soon have to deal with the inevitable need for income.

Before David's illness, David had been in complete control of our finances. He gave me a checkbook for our personal account. As long as I was conservative, I wrote checks to buy what the family needed without David interjecting any concern. This was the extent of my involvement in our finances. All I knew was David would go to work, build homes with his dad, and David would see to it we had enough money to cover our checks. It worked, so I asked no questions.

Chapter Eleven

After David's illness, this ignorance caused real problems. I was clueless as to where we stood financially. I assumed the money in our personal accounts was all we had available to us, and those funds were disappearing fast. I was unaware that in Eric's and David's business account was a great deal more of our money. David had been in the practice of withdrawing only the necessary funds to meet our immediate needs. The remaining money was held in the business account with the goal in mind of acquiring enough capital to someday build and own an apartment building without a mortgage. (Those resources weren't discovered until several years later when David resumed E & D Construction's bookkeeping.)

At the time of our financial trouble, I was not aware of the available money. Obviously, David did not remember it either. David's parents did not explain the situation because neither of them completely believed in David's amnesia. So when Eric asked me if I was all right or if I needed money, he was not offering charity as I had thought, he was asking if I needed any funds from the business that was half David's.

I was becoming more and more anxious about our cash-flow problem. I knew I needed to do something quick or we would be in desperate straits. But I was without an idea as to how to solve this problem. With three young children—which included one preschooler—as well as David needing help, I didn't know how I could get a job. We definitely couldn't afford a full-time baby-sitter, and David couldn't stay alone with Susan. And David, in his present condition, was not ready to go back to work. I was at a complete loss.

Pastor Buck came for another visit.

"David," he started. "I was really glad to see you at church on Sunday. It was wonderful. I looked down from the platform and there you were!" He smiled and paused, trying to find the right words to continue.

"For a long time now, I've been praying about some help at church." He paused again, this time with a thoughtful crease on his forehead. He cleared his throat and drew in a deep breath for courage.

"I have really enjoyed our prayer time together, David, and I was wondering if you would consider coming to the church in the mornings and praying there with me. Then maybe you could try getting a song together for the choir or just help with some odd jobs around the building. Just your being there to pray with me would help me immensely."

Awakened

David sat completely still, not moving a muscle, trying to assimilate what was being said.

Searching for words, Pastor Buck concentrated. A smile lit his face as his mind found the right words to express the way he was feeling.

"I am half a man, and you are half a man. . . . Maybe, together, we can make a whole man."

Tears came to my eyes as I saw David's eyes light up.

"Yes, I would like that," David responded.

"Wonderful," Walter expressed his joy at David's answer. Slowly, he turned toward me.

The compassionate smile he bestowed on me brought a lump to my throat. I swallowed and blinked my eyes as he continued.

"I was also wondering if you would be interested in being my secretary. I really need someone to help out on a part-time basis. It wouldn't pay much, but we would do something to compensate you for your time. I thought you might like to bring David in the mornings and, of course, Susan as well," he smiled. "And then go home whenever you need, maybe around lunchtime, or at least in time to get your other two girls."

A job! The possibilities swam through my mind at his words.

The Lord was providing a job right before my eyes. A perfect job. One with every obstacle overcome.

Walter's eyes lit up at the expression on my face. I'm not sure what he was seeing—awe, gratitude, relief, amazement, wonder, or disbelief. Maybe a bit of each, I don't know. But whatever he saw caused him to smile.

I stammered out a reply.

"Yes, I would love to be your secretary."

"Great," Pastor Buck responded, "How soon can you start?"

I thought ahead, quickly sifting through my immediate plans. Nothing stood in the way of starting right now.

"Tomorrow?" I tentatively suggested.

"Wonderful!" he bellowed as he stood up.

"I will see both of you tomorrow at, say, 9:00 A.M.?"

"Fine," I replied as I walked him to the door.

"See you tomorrow, then, and . . . thank you, Joan. I'm looking forward to working together with both you and David." He smiled as he walked through the door. As he was leaving, he turned back to me with

Chapter Eleven

a last parting comment. "You and David are the answer to my prayers, blessed ministers sent by God."

Pastor Buck's words touched my heart. *Blessed ministers?! . . . Sent by God?!* Could those words possibly apply to me and David? Yet our pastor had just spoken them to us. Could it be true?

I caught a glimpse of the reality that God really was sovereign. Everything I was going through was orchestrated by God—even the frightening, dark walk I was traveling. God was in control of my destiny, and He was in control of David's as well. I sensed a purpose and design in what was taking place. I wasn't sure what it was, but God had a mission for David and me—and He was going to make it clear to us. I was stunned by the thoughts racing through my mind. David and I were going to be helpers—ministers—in our church. Unbelievable but true.

The next day, David, Susan, and I showed up at Evangel Temple a few minutes before 9:00 A.M. We were excited and nervous, but Pastor Buck put us at ease from the start. I fit right in as secretary; my typing and mimeograph skills

Church office secretary Joan with "junior secretary" Susan by her side—1966

returned without any difficulty. David immediately closeted with Pastor Buck in his office for prayer before taking on other tasks around the building.

Pastor Buck asked David to lead the choir. David, growing stronger and bolder, said yes.

I was skeptical.

The first time he picked up a piece of music, he had no idea what it was, but he prayed and asked for help. David claimed the promise found

Awakened

in James: "If any of you lacks wisdom, let him ask of God, who gives to all liberally and without reproach, and it will be given to him" (James 1:5). David tapped into that promise. As he rehearsed the choir with music in front of him, only I was aware he was completely ignorant of the black markings on the paper that rested on the music stand. But Jesus knew, and David talked to Jesus, and Jesus helped him.

The next Sunday, David raised his hands to signal the choir and accompanist to get ready. He metered the rhythm with his right hand and cued the pianist with his left—a solid *intro*. At the proper moment, he signaled the voices to begin. He didn't miss any of the dynamic markings in the piece, his arms gestured widely for each crescendo. He even ended the musical selection with a wide sweep of his arms, circling, to perfectly close the ending fermata. *A miracle!*

From the soprano section of the choir, I glanced over the congregation. I wondered if they knew the magnitude of the miracle they had just witnessed. Tears stung my eyes. I was so proud of David; he had conducted magnificently. The excitement tingled in my toes as my eyes, once again, swept over the assembled crowd. A smattering of "Amens" touched my ears, but as I searched the faces of the listeners, I saw no evidence of any awareness of what had really happened. I turned my attention back to David, wondering how he was doing.

Now that the music was done and the last wisp of sound had dispersed into the atmosphere, David looked lost, as if unsure what to do. Sweat stood out on his brow, and I watched a bead of perspiration slide down his jaw. He closed his eyes, completely drained of energy. His hands were trembling, and he grasped the music stand a brief moment for support.

It was customary for the choir director to seat the choir before leaving the platform. And this is what was expected from David right now. David opened his eyes. He blinked and then blinked again. Nothing came to mind. No habit kicked into gear. He was at a loss; his mind blank. David turned and dragged his exhausted frame off the stage, leaving a bewildered choir in his wake.

I quickly took over, desperately trying to distract them from David's disorientation. Turning slightly, I raised my hand so it was in view of all choir members, then I slowly lowered it. The choir saw my signal, and we were seated. The service continued undisrupted.

Chapter Eleven

As I sat in the choir loft, I felt a familiar peace settle over me. Even with David's misguided actions in full view, I saw the victory, and I was overcome by the knowledge that God was in control. Miraculously, David had ministered. His hands, his arms, his body had moved with the anointing of the Holy Spirit. In the hand of the Ultimate Conductor, David had been the baton.

Ministry of Music

THE EVANGEL-TONES CHOIR

Our new Evangel-Tones Choir, organized this year, is comprised of approximately 25 C. A. age young people. This choir provides the music for the 7:00 P. M. evening service and for special events. Special numbers for the evening service are also provided by members of the Youth Choir. David Anderson is the director and Virginia Lee is the pianist for this choir. Rehearsals for the Youth Choir are held each Monday evening at 7:30 P. M.

THE CHANCEL CHOIR

The dedicated musical talents of some thirty five adult and college age members make the Chancel Choir a true Ministry of Music. Under the capable direction of David Anderson, together with accompaniment of Vonnie Langaker, pianist and May Dalan, organist, the Chancel Choir provides music for the 11:00 A. M. Sunday worship services and special musical programs throughout the year. Choir practice is held each Thursday evening at 7:30 P. M.

"Ministry of Music" page from Evangel Temple church directory

159

Awakened

For the first time since David had come home from the hospital, his life had meaning, purpose, and most importantly, a future.

Suddenly, the hauntingly familiar question of why had God chosen not to restore David's mind when He had so miraculously touched his physical body seemed absent. Amazingly, it wasn't important anymore.

God wasn't finished with David, and God wasn't finished with me!

> 'Twas a life filled with aimless desperation,
> Without hope, walked the shell of a man.
> Then a hand with a nail print stretched downward,
> Just one touch, then a new life began.
>
> And the old rugged cross made the difference,
> In a life bound for heartache and defeat.
> I will praise Him forever and ever,
> For the cross made the difference for me. [9]

Our first family portrait after David's illness. Taken for the church directory—1966

Chapter Twelve

Each day with David presented a fresh challenge as he slowly crept back to a seminormal existence. From one moment to the next I never knew what to expect. I was to expect the unexpected . . . and believe in miracles.

I did!

Every move David made was bathed in prayer—each step, every word. He tried to allow God to lead him step by step in a walk of dependence and faith in Jesus Christ. David listened for God's voice in even the smallest, most seemingly insignificant situation. And then, once he heard the instructions, he acted in faith and trust, never doubting or questioning the direction. David knew the One who had fought death and won—the One who had healed his physical body—was the same One in whom he could rely to lead him and to give him wisdom and knowledge at the exact, precise moment needed.

Amazingly, David and I began to live in another dimension—a life where, almost daily, miraculous things took place. And slowly, day by day, David peeled off more of the *Fragile: Handle with Care* sticker that had been slapped on his life by his illness.

In May 1966, about seven months after David "woke up," he decided it was time for him to drive a car again. But in the time since his illness, David's March birthday had passed and his driver's license had expired. We went to the Department of Licensing together with hopes of an easy, hassle-free renewal of his license. No such luck!

When we got there, we were informed that because too much time had lapsed for the standard renewal, David would be required to pass a written test before the license could be reissued. The only consolation was it would not be necessary to do a road test. Unfortunately, the road test was not the problem. David seemed to return quickly to some tasks he performed routinely prior to his illness; driving was one such task. The written exam, however, required his cognitive abilities. David's damaged memory would certainly not help him now.

The examiner showed David where to take his exam and, automatically, I began to follow. Her voice stopped me.

"Excuse me, Mrs. Anderson, but you will have to wait here."

What? . . . I can't go?

Images of David straining over the test questions, confused and disoriented, slammed into my mind. I was convinced David wouldn't be able to pass the examination without my help. I wasn't even sure if he would totally comprehend the test questions. I needed to communicate my concern to the employee. I swallowed, hoping for some inspiration to spill out of my mouth that would invoke her mercy.

"Would it be all right for me to go with him?" I implored. "I realize this request is unusual, but I need to make sure he understands the questions that are asked."

The employee looked at me as if I were an amateur con artist.

I hurried on.

"You see, David is recovering from a serious illness, and . . . and he has a little trouble comprehending things in writing," I stammered to a finish, hoping my petition would be granted. I leaned forward, eager for some compassion.

Chapter Twelve

"I'm sorry," she automatically responded. Then she hesitated, her glance shifting quickly to David, as if looking for conspicuous scars left behind by his disease. A sheen of nervous perspiration dotted David's brow, and his skin held a slight pallor.

Her voice turned apologetic as she continued. "No one is allowed to be with applicants while they are being tested. It is the standard rule, and we aren't allowed to break it."

I begged one more time. "Not even for a renewal? He only missed his expiration date by a couple months; his birthday was just last March. Can you bend the rule just this once."

"I'm sorry, ma'am," her voice was crisp. "If David is to drive a vehicle, he needs to be able to pass the state's written exam on his own."

Dismissing me with her words and a gesture, she turned to David and briskly quizzed him. "Do you want to take the examination?" She was all business.

"Yes," he matter-of-factly stated. Then he turned to me, and his lips lifted in a slight smile as he saw my defeated gaze.

"Don't worry, sweetheart," he reassured. "I'll be OK."

His hand reached out and touched my sleeve, and he leaned close to my ear.

"I won't be alone," he whispered.

I looked into his face, amazed by the confidence and trust which had displaced his nerves. He dropped my arm after a slight squeeze of affection, and he followed the examiner out of the room.

I watched David walk away. I was upset. I was tired of being the sole means of transportation in our home. I had really been looking forward to David being able to drive again. But now I felt defeated. I knew there was no humanly possible way for David to pass that test. I desperately tried to find even a small morsel of David's confidence, but couldn't. I knew there was an instinct David carried within him that would make him an adequate driver—just like he amazingly played the piano. I also knew that if asked specific questions of "how" and "why" and "when," David would be clueless. The monumental task of educating David once again of the rules of the road loomed large in front of me.

Not too much later, David came back wreathed in smiles.

"How did you do?" I hesitantly asked. My nerves were shot. I was trying desperately to be supportive.

"I passed," he announced.

"Passed?!" I said with shock.

"I got them all right. The lady said I got 100 percent."

My jaw dropped open. Dumbfounded, I stared at David.

David had passed. He *passed!* All of the questions answered correctly! No answers wrong. A miracle!

My head buzzed as I stood. Numbly, I walked with David back to the counter and the waiting clerk. She looked up as we drew near and smiled. Her smile held a hint of pity for David—not for his illness, but for having to put up with me, his apparently overprotective wife.

"Congratulations, Sir. You did real well." Her words were laced with pleasure and even a little pride in David's accomplishment.

"Thank you," David happily replied.

I stood silent as the remainder of the paperwork was completed. I kept repeating over and over in my mind, *This is the man that has trouble reading a menu in a restaurant to decide what to eat, and . . . and he has just gotten 100 percent on a driving exam? How?* It didn't make sense. I blinked my eyes, trying to clear my head of the conflicting thoughts rapidly flashing through my mind.

From a distance I heard the clerk spit out her well-rehearsed spiel of how long it would be before David received his permanent card in the mail. In a daze, I watched the delivery of David's temporary license to his hand, and before I knew it, we were heading for the exit; our trek a surprising success.

When we got to the car, David climbed behind the wheel. I watched him start the car, back it out of the parking stall and out to the street.

Well, his driving is fine, . . . but how did he pull off the mental stress test he just endured? I was still too stunned to voice my curiosity.

Once we got onto the main street, David turned to me with animated eyes.

"It was wonderful, sweetheart," he exclaimed. "Beautiful! You *should* have been there." His focus drifted back to the test.

"What?" I prompted, intrigued and fascinated.

David continued.

"Well, I got to the examining booth and read the first question." He paused slightly, remembering his agitation. "And, as you probably guessed," he laughed in a slight self-mocking tone, "I couldn't make heads or tails of it—something about a car coming one way and then

Chapter Twelve

another car comes or something—and they asked who has the right of way . . . or . . . I don't know, . . . something like that."

He shrugged his shoulders, dismissing the need for accurate recall, and continued.

"Anyway, I prayed right on the spot—and Jesus answered."

His head swung around to make eye contact.

"A light shone on the paper," he said matter-of-factly.

Then David's attention was seized by the traffic around him, and he hesitated. I waited impatiently for some sort of explanation to his words. Light doesn't just shine from nowhere onto someone's written test paper.

David maneuvered around the moving vehicles, and then, finally, resumed his recollection of the moment.

"I looked up to see where the light was coming from, but it was hard to tell. There was no source of the pin-light—no hole in the ceiling, no overhead bulb. It was just there, shining on my test, directly over an answer."

He glanced at me, faith and appreciation for his Savior sparkled in his eyes.

"So I circled the spot the light indicated and moved on to the next question."

He stated his faith act as if it were the most logical thing to do.

"As my eyes shifted to question number 2, the light also moved. This time it shown on a specific answer for that question, and I circled it."

David laughed again.

"Each time my eyes transferred to a new question, the light repositioned as well, picking out a different answer for each problem. And every highlighted answer the light gave me, I circled."

David stole another peak at my stunned face and smiled. Satisfaction and accomplishment mingled with faith and trust. He was happy about the license he now had in his possession, but at the same time, he knew from where it really had come.

"I guess the Lord wanted me to drive."

David getting his license became a mixed blessing for me. It was wonderful to be able to relinquish control of the wheel, but David became a little crazy with it. He was free and in control. He was a little like a teenager with a new toy. He obeyed traffic laws, but he was not all that cautious. He got into the car with one goal in mind: to get from one place to another and, of course, to see all the beautiful, God-created scenery in

Awakened

between. He was definitely not what one would call a defensive driver. David had complete trust the other guy would get out of his way.

Sometimes his fearless driving scared me senseless, and I would press my foot to the floor on an imaginary brake, clench my hands, and press my back into my seat, vainly trying to control the car from the passenger seat.

"Honey, watch out for that car!" or, "Honey! Slow down!" would explode from my mouth.

David would only laugh at my gasp and turn his head my way.

"Sweetheart, what's wrong?" he would inquire, seemingly oblivious of my tension.

"I don't want us to get in an accident," would be my obvious reply.

He would get a perplexed look on his face and say, "But then we would die . . . and get to go to heaven."

Without being able to quote the actual Scripture verse, David intuitively knew that to be suddenly absent from the steering wheel meant he would be present with the Lord.

He would laughingly exclaim, "Wouldn't that be great—to live in the Light?"

Not too long after David discovered his ability to play piano, he bravely took his violin out of the closet. I had told him about the lessons he had taken as a child, and about his musical background in high school and church. So, one day, armed with the encouraging miracle of his piano playing abilities and fueled by curiosity, David ventured to the closet. He opened the case and touched a string, plucking the tight line. A note sounded, and the sweet anticipation of musical pleasure teased his mind's ear.

He reached into the case and lovingly stroked the wood. Then he studied the violin, hoping for a smidgen of help from his memory, but nothing came. With his mind blank, he let his body take over. His hands began to move, mechanically reacting to a subconscious motivation. David picked up the instrument. The long piece of wood felt good in his left hand—comfortable, . . . at home.

Chapter Twelve

With his right hand he reached for the bow. The horsehair hung limp and lifeless. He didn't try to think, he just reacted. Moving down the length of the bow his hand stopped at the far point. He began to twist. The hairs bobbed up and down with David's manipulation, and they became taut.

He positioned the instrument under his chin, again confident he was doing the right thing, and drew the bow across the strings.

Vibrating melody emerged from the violin. David smiled; he liked what he heard.

Suddenly, the fingers of his left hand began to dance across the fingerboard as he plunged the bow out and back. Music burst from the wood in David's hand! The miracle melody was created by hands surrendered to his God.

David continued to relearn various things and generally did well. The process for him, however, was mentally taxing. Consequently, he would regularly become fatigued and, at times, weepy, as his emotional well would run dry.

Little things bothered him. Sentimental memorabilia really depressed him. At times, our house would feel oppressive to him, as though the weight of all the lost memories were crowding out the breathable air. Photographs that included David prior to his illness would place David in a time he could not know. Those pictures screamed unmerciful taunts at him. So treasured photo albums and lovingly filled picture frames were stored away.

The few images that remained in view were portraits taken of our girls as babies, but those were never discussed. Those were tolerated only because David was not in them, he could divorce himself from their significance. A picture would be somewhat acceptable if David didn't have to deal with the fact he was part of the memory represented by the photograph.

We never watched home movies. But on the rare occasions when the movie projector was used to satisfy the request of other family members, David would leave the room until the showing was over.

Awakened

If David happened to see a picture with himself in it, he would get frustrated—almost angry—because he felt he should remember it. The portrait was evidence of the obvious, gaping hole in his memory. He would almost punish himself, leaving the room in a sweat, feeling like an alien in someone else's body.

If the past was discussed too much, David would emotionally pull away, bewildered and frightened. Occasionally, he would ask questions, but most of the time he was quiet.

Memory! It all came down to that one word. I could see a picture, smell a flower, feel the chill of fall in the air—and those tangible things would spark a myriad of memories for me. Boats on the water would generate a brief glimpse of my first date with David; carnations would conjure up images of our wedding; even the physical characteristics of our girls would bring to mind the face or gesture of a relative. But I would remain silent. There were no more chances to say, "Remember when? . . ."

Noise continued to bother David. Sounds of children laughing and playing were an irritation. Any kind of loud noise would throb through his skull; his head would pound, and his fragile nerves would unravel. His hands would reach for his head, and his fingers would try to massage the pain away. He would sit quietly, in pain, trying his best to cope, not really sure how to fix the problem except by kneading the pressure points on his head. That posture became a warning sign for me. Spurred into action, I would try to douse the offending sounds.

The only noise David could tolerate was live music. Consequently, music became our main source of entertainment and expression. Singing was our pastime. Our girls learned the piano, and they each played an additional instrument. Any way to express music was acceptable, and it didn't matter how loud the music was—as long as the music praised the Lord. Ironically, we could sing as loud as we wanted, but talking was done in a whisper. And there was never a shout or a scream in the house.

The doctors' prognosis that David's memory would improve with time was not completely correct. David did remember how to do certain things, but the memory of his pre-illness life was never recalled. Slowly, we began to accept the fact that his memory was not going to return, and we adapted to living a life without making connections to our past.

Although it took a while, eventually I stopped anticipating David to return to the man I married, and I accepted the man he was. David's nature was different, so I learned the changes. David no longer called me "honey;" I was addressed as "sweetheart." He no longer tinkered with cars; he was completely ignorant of their mechanics. And David no longer yearned for the "great outdoors." Even his taste buds changed. He now liked onions and maraschino cherries—before his illness he would never touch them.

I was never self-conscious with David, I always treated him with respect. I guess the reason for this is I never stopped loving David. Love is *not* an emotion, love is a *commitment*. Our love and interdependence developed directly out of my commitment to David's recovery and his commitment to regain a normal life.

Neither one of us were sure how to communicate our mutual feelings of affection, but after many awkward moments, we found our way back toward oneness. The miracle was that we grew together and not apart. (Later, I was told some staggering statistics. Well over half of amnesia cases end in divorce, even when the amnesia is only partial. The number increases dramatically—close to 100 percent—when the amnesia is complete memory loss.) Our relationship balanced as I began to see wonderful new characteristics in the man to whom I was now married. And David saw me as a helpmate and friend.

Eventually, as day turned into year, I began to see more clearly the Living Christ directing David and moving through him, living in him. Loving this Christ-lead man became easy.

> I am crucified with Christ, nevertheless, I live;
> Yet not I, not I, but Christ liveth in me,
> Christ liveth in me.
>
> Oh glorious, wondrous, matchless truth, that in the Word I see;
> The risen Savior, glorified, lives out His life in me.
> I yield to Him and reckon self as crucified and dead,
> So that the life of Christ, my Lord, may be outlived instead.
>
> This is the path of power divine, for service here below;
> The only real effective way to count for God I know.

Awakened

> 'Tis by the Holy Spirit's power that He abides with me,
> And as I to His lordship yield, He gives me victory.
>
> Christ lives through me,
> Christ lives through me,
> By the Holy Spirit's indwelling power,
> Christ lives through me. [10]

In the early summer after his illness, David went back to work. Spring and summer are always busy months for construction work. Since David worked with his dad, he could work at his own pace, and Eric could keep an eye on David and instruct him whenever needed. Eric put no pressure on David to perform.

But when a subcontractor was temporarily on the job, the situation for David would be different. The subcontractors would give him no extra understanding—and definitely no room for error. David had graduated from the University of Washington with a degree in civil engineering, so he was expected to know technical details relating to the construction trade.

Every day, David would come home from work and lie down on the living room floor with his feet up on a chair. He would sleep, totally exhausted, until dinner. Then, after a quiet family meal, David would do a little paperwork or talk to his father on the phone.

At night, after we were in bed, I would ask David how his day had gone. Almost every night his answer would be a variation of a similar theme. Usually, his story would begin with the revelation of some problem or other that had arisen during the day that he had been forced to solve. Always, he had been uncertain of what to do. His never-failing first response would be to breathe a silent prayer, because God was always just a whisper away. Immediately, the answer would pop into his head.

In our bed, I would lay in the darkness, silently stretched out beside David, listening to the events of his day. I would hear about how he squared walls, laid out stairways, calculated roof angles, and handled other construction practices. Without fail, David would excitedly share how God had given him the knowledge for those common building tasks. The Lord would also give wisdom to solve problems that would be con-

Chapter Twelve

sidered difficult for *any* contractor. He would tell of subcontractors needing immediate, on-the-spot solutions, and then he would tell me how he had responded with a God-inspired answer.

Not long after David went back to work, property on Phinney Avenue in Seattle went on the real-estate market. David saw the property and immediately felt he should purchase it; it felt right, and he trusted that feeling. After the sale closed, miracles happened! Unforeseen, seemingly impossible things dropped from the sky.

David imagined the building he wanted to construct on the property. He took out a pencil and paper and began to draw what his mind saw. His hand moved over the graph paper, ruler and pencil working together to lay out the two-dimensional sketches of a seven-unit highrise. Amazingly, the ability to make the architectural drawings was in his hands. Engineering formulas and various concepts floated into his head: necessary load-bearing points, structural beam placement, ease of construction, economical design. . . .

David drew, and the solutions came. They popped into his head, divinely prompted. When he finished, he took his diagram to his father.

Eric barely looked at David's drawing. He was amazed, not at David's accomplishment, but at David's adventure in drawing a seven-unit complex for this particular lot.

"David," Eric tried to explain, "the property we own is only zoned for three units—no more. We would never be able to get permits for this building, let alone the funding. The maximum mortgage is only 60 percent of estimated cost, where are we going to get the other 40 percent?"

Eric's Swedish accent thickened with a little annoyance as he outlined the obvious obstacles. "I'm sorry, Son, but this is absolutely impossible."

Eric cleared his throat and patted David on the back, trying to soften the blow to David's creative effort. Eric's words had little impact on David's enthusiasm; he had seen the completed building in his mind. He knew it was possible, and he wasn't giving up without a fight.

"OK, Dad. If the property is only zoned for three units, then how do we change the zoning?" David attacked the heart of the problem.

Eric's eyes widened at the question. Startled, he laughingly replied, "Changing the zoning is impossible, David. Only the Building Department has the authority, but, as a rule, they don't change zoning."

"Well, we'll see," David persisted. "I'll go to the Building Department and see what they have to say. I won't believe we can't do this until I hear someone from the Building Department tell me it's impossible. I really believe God is in this—and I'm not ready to give up just yet."

David went to the Building Department and found the predominant zoning in the Phinney neighborhood was consistent with what Eric had said. Refusing to be discouraged, he researched the matter further. David discovered the city had randomly chosen a few lots in residential areas to be marked for larger, multiple-residence zoning. The chosen properties had been identified on the large sectional maps with red dots. He scanned through the maps and found the appropriate one for the Phinney Avenue neighborhood.

Right in the middle of unmarked properties lay two red dots: one on the corner lot adjoining David's property, and the other right in the middle of his lot. David's face broke out in a big grin, and he laughed.

"Well, I think I can build the seven-unit."

The permits were issued without a hitch, and construction began.

David's sketchy architectural drawings were followed; and amazing, time-saving and money-saving miracles resulted: All the spans were perfect—no joists had to be cut. Subcontractors commented that the building had been designed like a kit, ready to join without any fuss or modifications. The plumber's pipes flew right through, straight and direct, without any cost-eating adjustments. The plumber's job went together so smoothly he "kicked back" a percentage of his labor cost.

Sunray Apartments designed by David. Building on right was completed first, then second building was added with entry and elevator between—1969

The property on which E & D Construction was building the seven-unit was view property. Inexplicably, David had designed the plans to have a stairwell on the view side. This made no logical sense at all, and Eric tried to change David's mind. (David still shakes his head when he thinks about it now.) But David was adamant it was the way it was to be built. When man thinks *major mistake*, God makes a miracle.

Chapter Twelve

As it turned out, while they were finishing the building, the lot next door (the other "red dot") went on the market. The father-and-son team were able to purchase that property and build a nine-unit building on the adjoining property. They flip-flopped the plans—this time the windows facing the view. So when the nine-unit was completed next to the seven-unit, the stairwells of the two buildings mated perfectly, saving thousands of dollars. They ended up with a sixteen-unit complex spanning the two lots. Divine foreknowledge was the only explanation for that master plan.

During the construction of the nine-unit building on Phinney Avenue, David unexpectedly went out of town on a missionary trip to the Bahamas. He was called by Brother Gordon Weden, the head of the Mission America Placement Service Program (MAPS), which is an organization designed to help missionaries construct local churches. Gordon and his wife were friends of ours. In fact, Gordon was the contractor who had stepped in to finish the church David had been building when he was hospitalized.

Gordon phoned to see if David would be interested in helping out with a church building project MAPS was undertaking in the Bahamas. Gordon, like most people, knew of David's healing but didn't realize the extent of his memory loss. So when he asked David to "help out," he had nothing less in mind than to have David be the general contractor.

David, not realizing the full extent of what would be expected of him, quickly agreed. He was always eager to do anything to help Jesus' church. He finished the conversation, hung up the phone, and turned to me.

"I'm going to help Gordon Weden build a church in the Bahamas," he informed me. He hesitated slightly, then questioned, "Where's the Bahamas?"

After a shocked minute or two, I explained. Then David prepared to go.

With the Phinney Avenue project underway, it was not a good time to leave, but David couldn't say no to God's work. The funds for the trip were supplied, and God gave David the wisdom needed to supervise the construction of the church. In turn, God took care of everything, including the project on Phinney Avenue.

Awakened

While David was gone, a fellow contractor came by the job site. He told Eric he had a project that was hung up waiting on permits. He could see E & D Construction's project had been framed in and was ready for drywall, and so he wondered if Eric wanted the help of his men. He would rather see his crew working for their wages instead of just sitting around.

Eric accepted the offered help. And when David returned, the building was farther along than it would have been if he had stayed home and worked twenty-four hours a day.

Similarly, other subcontractors were hurting for business, and they were willing to do work for a fraction of the regularly charged rate. This was a time in the economic history of the Northwest when the common one-liner was: "Would the last one out of Seattle please turn out the lights."

David in his element

The maximum mortgage the bank would lend David was 60 percent of the estimated cost of building the complex. When the building was finished, the books showed the complete project was constructed for only 55 percent of the estimated cost—an unbelievable accomplishment!

The entire project on Phinney Avenue was one

Addition to Sunray Apartments in full swing—1987

Chapter Twelve

miracle after another. The miracles even continued years after the completed construction. The weight-bearing foundation beams required by David's original design were considered too "beefy" for the intended three-story building with basement. But the subcontractors, of course, followed the design regardless of their own personal feelings on the subject. As a result, years later David was able to build an additional fourth story on the complex without strengthening the support. The building had originally been designed to carry the extra weight.

That kind of foresight is not available to the natural mind of man. There was no way David could have known the corner property would become available for purchase or that E & D Construction would be able to buy it. Nor

David in front of Sunray Apartments with penthouse addition—1988

was the idea of a fourth story penthouse even remotely in David's thinking when he drew the plans. Only God could have ordered those events, and it was accomplished through a man who is tapped into God's knowledge and had childlike faith to act on what he heard.

David taught his method for success to his children. Susan once asked her dad how he knew what was the right thing to do. David answered, "I pray and ask Jesus to help me, and He gives me the answers. If I forget to ask God for help and try to do something in my own strength, I fall flat on my face."

To this day, if David is confronted with a problem, he prays and trusts God for the answer. Then, in his own words, "The answer pops in

Awakened

his head." Faith—not only a belief in the existence of God, but also a complete and total reliance upon Him.

> What a fellowship, what a joy divine,
> Leaning on the everlasting arms;
> What a blessedness, what a peace is mine,
> Leaning on the everlasting arms.
>
> What have I to dread, what have I to fear,
> Leaning on the everlasting arms?
> I have blessed peace with my Lord so near,
> Leaning on the everlasting arms.
>
> Leaning, leaning, safe and secure from all alarms;
> Leaning, leaning, leaning on the everlasting arms. [11]

In 1970, about one year after the completion of the Phinney Avenue project and five years after David's illness, I had quite a shock: I was pregnant. Unexpectedly, my world was turned upside down again. I already had three children—counting David it sometimes seemed like I had four. I definitely had not planned on increasing the count.

David and I disagree with how this time in our life actually unfolded. He remembers wanting another child prior to my pregnancy; a child to remember growing inside my womb and one that he could hold as an infant and watch grow to adulthood. I, on the other hand, remember the emotions he describes came *after* our child was born.

I was terrified and felt way too old. In 1970, a thirty-three-year-old mother-to-be didn't seem to be the norm. I had an emotional struggle the entire nine months I was pregnant. I had never considered things like David being able to experience the arrival of a child, or to watch the child grow, learning to walk and talk and sing. I forgot our other children's early childhood had been ripped away from his memory, just as much as his own had been.

But God saw and understood, even when David and I didn't. Besides, when God quite literally drops a miracle into your lap, you accept it—and, hopefully, learn to say "thank you." In December 1970, our miracle, Scott David Eric Anderson, was born.

Chapter Twelve

I remember lying in the hospital room, crying. After having three daughters, I was comfortable raising girls. When a son was born, the only coherent thought in my befuddled brain was, *What are we going to do with a boy?*

Then the nurse came in.

"I have never seen a prouder father in all my years as a nurse," she bubbled. Her face beamed as she continued. "Your husband is walking two feet off the ground, and his face is literally glowing with pride. He's telling everyone he meets that he finally has a son."

Her words eventually registered with me, and after struggling with mountains of disbelief, I dried my tears.

David was completely thrilled to be the father of a newborn son. Of course, once we got Scott home, David had no idea what to do with a baby. Scott fascinated and captivated him and, at the same time, completely baffled him.

I had lots of willing hands to help, though, with three young girls ready to play with their new doll. David occasionally stepped in just to watch.

Family portrait with the addition of Scott—1971: David, 35; Joan, 33; Doreen, 14; Donna, 10; Susan, 8; Scott, 8 months

As the years have passed, I have thanked God many times for His special gift to us, our son, Scott. His smiles, his laughter, and his music have become a very precious blessing to us. God works in mysteriously wonderful ways.

In the summer of 1973, David got another phone call from Brother Gordon Weden—this time to help on a church building in Panama. Again David said yes.

Not long after the phone conversation, David was on a plane to Panama. While in the air, he closed his eyes to rest. In his mind, he saw a building. Then his view became clearer and more specific. In his vision he went inside the building to a specific room: a kitchen. All the fixtures were in perfect place. The floor plan was laid out in front of him, properly calculated and completely functional. Then the vision faded, and he became aware of his surroundings once again.

When the plane landed in Panama, David and the team were taken to the church. As they drove up to the building, David was stunned at what he saw. He was looking at the building of his vision. He gawked at the structure, but no one seemed to notice.

In short order, the team was given a tour of the entire project. As they entered the kitchen-to-be area, their guide started explaining some of the logistical problems they were facing. The room was empty, and they were having a terrible time designing a functional kitchen within the limited space provided. That phase of the project was at a complete standstill, and they desperately needed help.

David looked around the bare room, and he could see in his mind's eye the layout from his vision. It would fit exactly. The vision he had been given on the plane was the solution to the problem the men in Panama were facing. He could contain his excitement no longer. David shared his vision with the crew, and they were astonished. The job was miraculously completed in record time.

David standing in kitchen designed for church in Panama—1973

>Take my life and let it be,
>Consecrated, Lord, to Thee,
>
>Take my hands . . .
>Take my feet . . .
>
>Take my voice and let me sing
>Always, only, for my King.

Chapter Twelve

> Take my lips and let them be
> Filled with messages for Thee.
>
> Take myself and I will be
> Ever, only, all for Thee. [12]

David put his life in God's hands, and God used him. Whether it was a request for construction or engineering help or ministry in music, David always said yes to the call. This willingness to serve took him around the globe: Africa, Bahamas, Costa Rica, Germany, Hawaii, Indonesia, Japan, New Zealand, Norway, Panama, Sweden—and the list goes on.

David on a missionary trip to Africa—1982

David on a missionary trip to Costa Rica—1991

Awakened

> Blessed Assurance, all is at rest.
> I in my Savior, am happy and blessed.
> Watching and waiting, looking above,
> Filled with His goodness, lost in His love.
>
> This is my story,
> This is my song,
> Praising My Savior all the day long;
> This is my story,
> This is my song,
> Praising my Savior all the day long. [13]

David had a dream.

He desired to expand his ministry of music. He was still involved in our church's music ministry, but he felt it was time to branch out evangelistically. He sensed the Lord wanted to use him with his family to give testimony to the healing and sustaining power of Jesus Christ. David believed that as God's knowledge and power worked through us, we would become tools in His hand. He also knew every time we met an audience we would be completely dependent upon God to work through us. And then, God, the source and the strength of our ministry and our life, could use our family to bring glory to His name.

In the mid-1970s, David's dream became a reality. The Horizon Sounds by the Anderson Family was formed. Scott would sit on the bench while the girls, David, and I ministered together in concert. Then David would share our story.

David's dream unfolded: a dream of music, of family, of praising Jesus in song and testimony.

Epilogue

I sat staring into the space of the gymnasium, only slightly aware of the people around me. I vaguely recalled that the awards had been passed out and our family had sung to the large gathering. As David brought his testimony to a close, the undeniable truth penetrated my mind, the meaning of David's words: *David had not known me.*

The pieces of the puzzle were finally fitting together. The images of my memory were rejoining to form a familiar picture with new clarity. I had been a stranger to David, a stranger just like everyone else in his new world. He had been totally alone, without any frame of reference, *completely* without memory.

I tried to focus on David's words. He was telling of the goodness of Jesus, of His wonderful restorative healing power. He was going to tell about the plans we had—to make an album and tour the United States.

Yet, I could not escape the revelation I had just received: David had not known me. This was *so* hard to believe. But as I looked back, I couldn't understand how I could have been so blind. I had known David didn't remember his mother and father or any of his other relatives. David also had not known our children. And I had known David could not even remember who *he* was. Yet, somehow, in all the chaos of our pain, incredibly, inconceivably, and illogically, I never fully grasped the fact he didn't remember *me*.

Epilogue

I sat stunned.

How was it even possible I could have overlooked the blatant fact David did not remember me? I had assumed somewhere, hidden in his heart, his love for me had survived the onslaught of his illness. I felt like I had found the last piece of a puzzle, I could finally see the entire picture. I knew now David's love for me had *not* survived his illness.

His instant trust in me that day in the hospital had masked our interrupted relationship. For the first time I realized that in David's mind he had, without ceremony, "married" me when the doctor whispered into his ear, "That young lady is your wife." That was his wedding day. The miracle was that he placed his trust in me, a stranger. From that trust a new love grew in his heart for me.

Our love was strong because it had faced immediate and hard challenges, strong because it had grown in the midst of a violent storm.

David and Joan's twenty-fifth wedding anniversary.—August 1980
They renewed their vows in a ceremony David could remember

I reflected on the incredible things that had happened to David and me, the inconceivable emotions that had been my day-to-day existence: David sitting alone crying; David's total dependence on Jesus, his sole Friend; David uncomfortable with any human contact; David not sure when to touch; David sitting alone in our darkened living room. I

Epilogue

thought, *Why now?* Why am I beginning to understand the full significance of David's amnesia now?

Unbidden, the words flooded my questioning mind, *"Because, My child, now you are able to bear the knowledge."*

I sat paralyzed in my seat. I was jolted yet comforted by the words. *Jesus.* How marvelously wonderful is the voice of Jesus. The Word of God I had quoted many times before filled my heart, "God will not allow you to be tempted beyond what you are able . . . to bear" (I Cor. 10:13). The words now held new meaning for me.

I closed my eyes, and quietly the tears slipped from beneath my lashes. God had kept the full magnitude of David's memory loss from me to shield me, to protect me. David as a stranger to our children, our family, our home, and our past had been devastating enough. But somehow, in God's mercy, I had been blind to my own strangeness. Christ had spared me from the deepest, most mind-shattering, most debilitating knowledge of David's condition when my vulnerability had been at its lowest point. He had held back an undeniable and completely logical aspect of David's amnesia from my understanding until I had gained sufficient strength to bear the truth. The Lord knew I was now stronger. David was stronger. We were healed.

Now, higher than ever, I would lift up my voice to God, my Source and my Strength, and praise His name for sparing me. I had received mercy. Therefore, I would sing praise to the One who showed mercy—my God and Savior, Jesus Christ.

Years have passed since David's illness. We did record several music albums, and we even toured the United States as a singing family. Our children are grown, and they are all married to wonderful Christians. God stepped into each one of their lives and held them through the confusing years of David's illness. He wiped out wounds of hurt and confusion that could have festered and poisoned the rest of their lives. Jesus set them free, then molded each one into who He desired.

Every one of our children has music woven into their lives, and we still enjoy making music together. David says, "The family that sings together, stays together." This is true, especially when the singing involves praise to Jesus Christ, our Savior.

Epilogue

Record album cover; first recording of The Anderson Family—1976

Praising Him also helps restore damaged relationships. When Helen became too frail to live on her own, David and I took her into our home. We acted according to the Word of God where it reads, "Honor your father and mother," and we trusted God to help us in caring for her.

Every morning she and I sat at our kitchen table with our cups of coffee and we conversed. We talked, we laughed, we prayed, and at times, we

Family portrait—1997. *Back row, left to right:* Susan, Scott, Alison (Scott's wife), Joan, David, Doreen, Roy (Doreen's husband), and Donna. *Seated, left to right:* John (Susan's husband), and Sam (Donna's husband). *Front, left to right:* Ben, Tyler, Heather, Holly, Sandra, Jeremy, Keith, and Jessica.

Epilogue

sang praises to Jesus. Remarkably, we began to accept and appreciate each other. I can't tell you how much that meant to me. Miraculously, our relationship grew into a friendship that lasted until the day she died. Praise the Lord!

Bringing glory to God's name is the purpose for our existence. This is the reason David was healed. God has the power to immediately relieve suffering and sorrow from our lives, but He also holds our greatest good *and* His glory as the ultimate goal. God Almighty reached down and touched David's body with His all-powerful, healing hand. Yet, in His infinite wisdom, He left David's mind without memory.

Why God chose to do that is beyond my comprehension. I might as well ask why Jesus, in John, chapter 5, healed only one man at the pool of Bethesda. The pool was surrounded by a multitude of sick, blind, and lame people. Every one of them was in desperate need of a touch from the Savior's hand. Why did He choose to touch just one man? Or I might ask why Shadrach, Meshach, and Abednego were saved from being consumed in a fiery furnace yet remained captive in Babylon?

Were those deeds half done? No! God is sovereign.

Did those miracles bring glory to God? Yes! Sometimes God allows a child of His to endure physical illness or suffering for His glory. Jesus didn't rush to the side of ailing Lazarus. He postponed his arrival until Lazarus was dead. But then the glorious life-giving power of Jesus was revealed through the consequent miracle.

David's memory remains badly crippled and frequently unclear. The damaged portion of his brain continues to delete memory every day. For example, if David tries to read a book, by the time he has reached the end of a page, he finds it impossible to remember what he read at the beginning of it. Almost daily, David is confronted with a situation that could escalate into a real crisis because of his lack of recall. At those times, Jesus is the storehouse for his mind—his source of information. David relies on God, and his dependence leads to God's provision of health, strength, and knowledge. Step by step, moment by moment, day by day, David, by just being alive and having complete reliance on Almighty God, brings glory to the name of Jesus Christ.

Epilogue

David and Joan ministering in song, on tour in Norway—1989

Through the years I have learned all too well David and I are not alone in experiencing difficulties in life. In fact, being a Christian does not automatically exclude a believer from difficulties. Pain and sadness are all around us, but that unidealistic reality only opens the door for God to flood us with His unconditional love and support. Jesus promised to always be with us in every circumstance, even through the Valley of the Shadow of Death, when the darkness of night seems impenetrable and unending.

David and I believe God has gracious control of our lives and He will be faithful to direct our path and give us what we need to walk through life's unpredictable days. In submission and humility, we lay down all our finite questions at the feet of Jesus, and believe He has our good and His glory as the ultimate conclusion of His divine plan.

We are vessels being formed in Jesus' hand. He isn't finished with us, but He has promised to complete what He has started. Now that is a miracle! And one day each of our vessels will be whole, beautiful, and unmarred—perfect in every way, and all to the glory of the Master Artist.

Praise the name of Jesus!

Whenever I have the opportunity to tell our story, I close with Psalm 66 TLB. It is our testimony; it is our life.

> Sing to the Lord, all the earth!
> Sing of his glorious name!
> Tell the world how wonderful he is.

Epilogue

> How awe-inspiring are your deeds, O God!
> How great your power!
> All the earth shall worship you and sing of your glories.
>
> Come, see the glorious things God has done.
> What marvelous miracles happen to his people!
>
> Let everyone bless God and sing his praises,
> for he holds our lives in his hands.
> And he holds our feet to the path.
>
> We went through fire and flood.
> But in the end, you brought us into wealth and great abundance.
>
> Come and hear, all of you who reverence the Lord,
> and I will tell you what he did for me:
> For I cried to him for help,
> with praises ready on my tongue.
> He would not have listened
> if I had not confessed my sins.
> But he listened!
> He heard my prayer!
> He paid attention to it!
>
> Blessed be God who didn't turn away when I was praying,
> and didn't refuse me his kindness and love.

Whatever is in the past, whether remembered or forgotten, in Christ it ceases to matter. Jesus restores and builds a life in the present and toward a future. David's future burns bright as he walks in constant communication with Jesus. Moreover, my own future holds no fear. Soon, in Christ, time shall be no more. David and I lean on the passage from Isaiah 43:18–19*a* which reads, "Cease to dwell on days gone by and to brood over past history. Here and now I will do a new thing."

Acknowledgments

1 "No More Death," Copyright © 1972 by John W. Peterson Music Company. All rights reserved. Used by permission.

2 "Really Live," Copyright © 1971 by John W. Peterson Music Company. All rights reserved. Used by permission.

3 "Blessed Assurance," Crosby/Knapp.

4 "Give Them All to Jesus," by Phil Johnson and Bob Benson Sr. Copyright © 1975 by Multisongs—a division of Careers-BMG Music Publishing, Inc. (SESAC) All rights reserved. Used by Permission.

5 "What a Friend," Scriven/Converse.

6 "Brokenness," by David Meece, Dwight Liles, Mike Hudson, Niles Borop. Copyright © 1993 Ariose Music/Meece Music/ N. B. Music. Used by permission.

7 "His Eye is on the Sparrow," Martin.

8 "Praise the Lord," Brown Bannister/Mike Hudson/Word Music (100%)/ASCAP. Copyright © 1978 Word Music, Inc. All RIghts Reserved. Used by permission.

Acknowledgments

9 "The Old Rugged Cross Made the Difference," words by William J. and Gloria Gaither. Music by William J. Gaither. Copyright © 1970 Gaither Music Company ASCAP. All rights controlled by Gaither Copyright Management. Used by permission.

10 "Christ Lives Through Me," Copyright © 1972 by John W. Peterson Music Company. All rights reserved. Used by permission.

11 "Leaning on the Everlasting Arms," Showalter/Hoffman.

12 "Take My Life and Let it Be," Havergal/Peterson.

13 "Blessed Assurance," Crosby/Knapp.

To order additional copies of

Awakened

send a donation of $12.99 plus $3.95 shipping and handling to

The Horizon Sounds
4207 Phinney Ave. N. #D
Seattle, WA 98103

If you would like to write David and Joan Anderson, or have them speak to your church or group, they can be contacted at the above address or through e-mail (daja1@juno.com).